Stumbling Toward Applause

Best wishes, Dal

Doug Matthews

gearsixcreative

Other Books by Doug Matthews

How to Create Fantasies and Win Accolades:
A Practical Guide to Planning Special Events

Special Event Production: The Process

Special Event Production: The Resources

Stumbling Toward Applause:
Misadventures
in Entertainment

Doug Matthews

Cover Design: Ted Couling

Library and Archives Canada Cataloguing in Publication

Matthews, Doug, 1946-   Stumbling toward applause : misadventures in entertainment / Doug Matthews.

ISBN 978-0-9733987-4-8

        1. Matthews, Doug, 1946- --Anecdotes. 2. Special events--Planning--Anecdotes. 3. Special events--Anecdotes. I. Title.

GT3406.C3M38   2012   394.2692   C2012-901908-9

Published by:

Gear Six Creative
1104 – 288 Ungless Way
Port Moody, B.C. V3H 0C9
Canada

E-mail: gear6@shaw.ca

"Anyone who tries to make a distinction between education and entertainment doesn't know the first thing about either."

Marshall McLuhan

Contents

Acknowledgments

I owe a debt of gratitude to the man who got me started in the entertainment business, Ben Kopelow. For four years, he was my partner and mentor before he decided to retire.

During those years, I learned from a master who entrusted me with his tremendous wealth of knowledge. A true entrepreneur and creative thinker, he made a fascinating teacher. Thank you, Ben.

I must also acknowledge the talented performers and suppliers who worked with us over the years. I felt honoured to have you as enthusiastic members of our team.

Likewise, thanks must go to the hundreds of thousands of guests who attended our events and shows. Your applause made everything worthwhile.

Everyone is important on this list, and none more so than my wife, Marimae. She endured countless nights over the course of my career when I would awaken her at the witching hour having survived yet another event and wanting so much to relate to her my tales of woe or success. She happily and patiently listened, which is all I could ask.

Introduction

Warming Up the Audience

Thunderous applause. Connecting with the audience. It's the goal of every performer. In my job as the person responsible for planning private corporate entertainment shows as part of special events, and putting the right performers onstage at the right time, it was also *my* goal and a measure of *my* success. Unfortunately, something happened along the way.

Jungle animals on the loose, bar fights, pyrotechnics gone awry, technical glitches, unusual brushes with the famous, a sweltering outdoor show for UN troops in war-torn Cambodia, and clients who committed deadly sins—

these are but a small sampling of the stories that await within this book.

This is more than a memoir. A narrated personal history, which would be far too egocentric, is not my style. Rather, the book is the product of reflection, a reflection that has revealed lessons learned in the course of a career through the observation of human nature. In my case, that career was in the field of entertainment, for a short time as a musician, and for a longer time as both an entertainment agent and a special event producer. It roughly covers the time from the early 1980s to 2004, a period when what is now known as the "special events industry" was in its infancy.

When I started out in the business in Vancouver, Canada, after a first career in the Canadian Armed Forces, the term "special event" was virtually unknown. Before then, people used to attend such events—as they have done since prehistory—but they were called affairs, dinners, parties, functions, dances, ceremonies, and such. By around the mid-1980s, large national and international conferences and corporate meetings were becoming increasingly popular, and a big part of these gatherings were smaller events like opening ceremonies, stage shows, and theme dinners. All of these required some form of entertainment. Luckily, our company was well placed to provide such entertainment. Founded by my partner Ben Kopelow in 1961, the company had previously been booking mainly bars and nightclubs, but once these "special events" took hold, we followed the money. Our talent roster, with its dance bands, singers, comedians, jugglers, magicians, caricaturists, and other variety acts, turned out to be a perfect fit.

However, this new industry required *more* than just straightforward bookings. It demanded creativity in the form of unique shows that presented entertainment in untested forms and combinations. Long before I arrived on the scene, Ben had been pioneering these kinds of creative shows and theme events for corporate clients. As a founding member of the Barnstormers, one of Vancouver's original professional theatre companies, and as the first theatrical booking agent in the city in the early 60s, he used his love of theatre and a creative bent to do things nobody else had done. Emerging from his fertile brain came lavish affairs that combined spectacular décor with unusual presentations of entertainment and dinner. For example, one of the favourite theme events in Vancouver for his clients was called a "Forest Night," designed to evoke the Canadian wilderness—indoors and minus the mosquitoes. Ben would completely envelop a hotel ballroom with literally hundreds of live, twenty-foot-tall evergreen trees and thrill guests with live grizzly bears, moose, deer, cougars, and eagles, all close enough to touch. Then he would stage a show with real loggers competing in axe throwing, chopping, buck sawing, and tree climbing, long before it was done anywhere else in North America for the public. The word of these spread and soon clients were constantly demanding more and more outlandishly creative events. Our mandate was to enthrall audiences. To do so, we often took chances in what was then a virtually unregulated industry with minimal concern for risk. This was the enjoyable part for me and the part that yielded the majority of stories in this book.

The stories begged to be written. They begged to be written not because of any overwhelming desire on my part to impress people, but because in the course of more than ten years of giving lectures and teaching about special event planning and production, my students and audiences just could not get enough of my real experiences in the field. Without exception, whenever I regaled them with some crazy anecdote and related it to the topic I was discussing at that moment, everyone came alive.

I don't know if it's just human nature to enjoy the sufferings of others, but the popularity of reality TV would indicate that it probably is. A lot of these stories are at my own expense, so reading them is a little like reality TV; you just have to use your imagination a bit more. I probably would not have written such revealing stories had I still been in business. As you will notice, however, I was not always the only person with a red face. Everyone in the book is real, except that some names have been changed or only first names used for reasons that will soon become obvious.

I hope that you will find *Stumbling Toward Applause: Misadventures in Entertainment* an enjoyable read, one that reveals under the surface some nuggets of wisdom and lessons about life, business, and relationships.

Doug Matthews
Vancouver, Canada
January 2013

Chapter One

Suite 316

It was a quirky piece of architectural humour. A collection of matronly stone nurses glowered disapprovingly across Vancouver's Georgia Street from the exterior corners of the Georgia Medical Dental Building. As if in defiance, perched atop the Hotel Vancouver across the street, several grey gargoyles ogled back. I always wondered who would win this decades-long stony faceoff. According to recent news, it was going to be the gargoyles. Despite lively public protest, the wrecking ball was soon to render into dust the ugly example of 1929 art deco that was the nurses' home.

As I was thinking of this, I walked into the medical building under the glare of the nurses. I was on a mission to acquire a new job in entertainment. I had grown tired of my air force job, working in the snow of eastern Canada, and Vancouver held the tropical promise of a better life. I somehow knew this building held the key to that promise. Here also resided one of several non-medical entities, a reputable entertainment agency that I had heard about. It was on the third floor, suite 316 to be exact.

I waited while the cranky elevator bounced to a stop. There was no question this building and the various parts of its anatomy had seen their day, much like the few remaining doctors still practising here. Inside the lift, we—a collection of doctors, presumably, and nervous patients—rumbled upwards for about five minutes. The brass doors finally opened on the third floor. I got out, alone.

My god, I thought, this is 1930s vaudeville and I'm trapped in a time warp. The floor was mottled grey granite, the kind on which stilettos and good Italian loafers signal their approach with clicks and clacks. It wound around a quadrangle of offices, each with a smoky glass and polished mahogany door, each with a company name in black Broadway font emblazoned on the glass.

I clacked my way to 316. This was it. "Pacific Show Productions, proprietor Ben Kopelow." I opened the door half expecting a clown or overweight German accordionist in lederhosen to push past me. Close. I was greeted by "the secretary," vintage 1932 Hollywood—tight blue dress, inch-long red fingernails, shoulder-length red hair, and yes, stiletto heels. She was tapping away calmly on an IBM Selectric, only her fingernails hitting the keys.

She stopped and looked up with a smile, her blue eyes sparkling. "Hi, you must be Mr. Matthews."

"Absolutely right. I'm here to see Mr. Kopelow."

"Glad to meet you. I'm Kathy. I'll let his nibs know you're here."

Nothing quite like a good old-fashioned boss-secretary relationship, I thought.

I looked around the small reception area. All the pre-requisites were there: filing cabinets, two slightly worn guest chairs, Kathy's desk, the Selectric, a black phone (buttons, not a dial; aha, something modern), some colourful paintings of the Australian outback that seemed oddly out of place, and of course a coffee pot. Basic. Certainly not ostentatious.

Kathy emerged from the inner sanctum. "You can go in now."

The door was open a crack. I pushed it further. The office was bigger than I had imagined. The sun had managed to squeeze itself into the only visible patch of sky outside between the Art Gallery and the Eaton's store. Its rays were slashing through a haze of smoke that descended from the ceiling of the office. I glanced around quickly. Another Australian painting, a large one of Ayers Rock, hung above a beige couch at one end of the room. I was now truly curious, wondering what the Australian wilderness had to do with entertainment.

I walked through the haze to the other end of the room where "his nibs" sat, the "Grand Inquisitor" behind his immense mahogany desk, waiting to pounce on terrified sinners.

He remained seated but extended his hand. "Ah, the famous Doug Matthews. Have a seat."

"Great to be back in Vancouver, Mr. Kopelow, and to meet you after our conversations on the phone," I said as my face finally lowered below haze altitude and I could see his.

Another time warp. Sitting in front of me was Groucho Marx—at least the spitting image. No east-side New York accent, and the cigar had been replaced with a day-long chain of Du Maurier regulars, but Groucho nevertheless. Black horn-rims framed his relentlessly moving eyes.

"I hear you want to get into show business. And don't call me Mr. Kopelow. It's Ben," he puffed, dispensing with preliminary niceties as he butted out half his cigarette in a giant pink ashtray, almost overflowing. This was long before the era of smoke-free offices. Grinning and bearing it was a way of life, or death, depending on how long you could tolerate it.

"I do, and I want to do it in Vancouver where it doesn't snow. Your company seems to have a very professional approach. I thought I should visit and have a chat. Can you tell me a little more about the acts you book and where the company works?" In truth, the "professional approach" had been assumed on my part because of viewing a well-laid-out company Yellow Pages ad. This was the full extent of my homework. I really did need an answer to my question or I was lost.

The bushy eyebrows rose in mock surprise as he took another drag. "We do convention work mostly, the crème de la crème of entertainment. Clients pay on time and percentages are higher than bars. Here's a roster of some of our acts." He handed me four pages of typewritten descriptions with some grainy black and white photos. Jumping from the pages came "Tom Powell, the Millionaire Pickpocket," "The Amazing Jozef—Magic with a Snake," "Wes Harrison—Mr. Sound Effects," "Jose Gonzalez Gonzalez—Mexican Comedian," "Gillian Campbell and the Gold Nugget Dancers," and "Princess White Buffalo—Indian Fortune Teller," among others. For some reason, visions of Ed Sullivan skittered through my head.

"And we represent Rolf Harris when he's in Canada. I've just finished a long tour with him, all over the place. That's why I couldn't see you before now." This was impressive. I remembered Rolf Harris, when, as a child, I mentally first helped him to tie down his kangaroo. That was a long time ago.

"He's still around?"

"Of course, and going strong. He puts on an incredible show—sings all his hits *and* paints a complete Australian scene. That's one of his paintings." Ben pointed to Ayers Rock at the other end of the office. "We usually sell out." OK, now the paintings made sense. I was becoming more impressed. A genuine star in the roster.

He took a final gasp of the second cigarette before adding it to the ashtray. "We also produce the theatre in Barkerville, the old gold rush town. Two original shows every summer. We're right in the middle of putting the final touches on this year's offerings." The word "we" struck me as a little incongruous at this point as I had only counted two people in the office. Not that this workload was impossible. It was just that I was still employed by her majesty's Canadian Armed Forces and the work ethic of private enterprise had not quite sunk in. It seemed this might be an opportune time to pop the question.

"Wow! Sounds like you have a lot going on. You could probably use some help, and that's really why I'm here. Entertainment fascinates me. I used to moonlight as a musician and I've always enjoyed it. Also, what you've described fascinates me. I'd like to join your company. You've read my resume. I think I could make a pretty substantial contribution."

"No, I'm not really looking for anyone. Tried another employee a couple of years ago. He didn't work out. I like to be independent." A new cigarette appeared, followed by an arrogant puff. Groucho had passed his temperament on to his clone. Ben seemed set in his ways.

I kept my cool. "I'm wondering why you agreed to see me then?"

"I just like to keep my eyes and ears open to who's new in town. Sorry, I don't think it's going to happen. But good luck in your job search."

"Yeah, thanks for seeing me." I was perturbed. Several long distance phone calls and letters had seemed to signal a good possibility of a job. Ben had not been as cooperative as anticipated.

He took a final gasp and exhaled a smoke ring around his parting insult, "Don't be a stranger."

As I left, Kathy chirped, "Sorry about that. You caught his nibs on a bad day. He's pooped from touring with Rolf. Seriously, call us again after you've talked to other companies while you're out here."

"Sure," I said, certain that would never happen. I walked out of the hazy outback, away from vintage Hollywood, vaudeville, and art deco, and exited under the now smiling nurses into a glorious Vancouver spring morning.

Little did I know.

Chapter Two

The Old Showman

Two days and two sleepless nights later, I returned. I still don't know why. Maybe it was the spring sunshine; maybe it was the compelling attraction of working in entertainment; or maybe I just liked musty art deco offices.

"So, you're back." Ben looked up from his writing, vaguely amused, as I trotted in.

"Yeah, I had trouble sleeping and I've done a lot of thinking," I said, standing in front of his leviathan desk.

"Do tell." He dragged on his cigarette, eyes rolling under the twin forests of eyebrows.

"You said you didn't want an employee, and I really want to be in show business. Before I go back to Ottawa, I want to make you an offer. What do you think if I throw in some money and we get a basic partnership going?"

He took a second drag and looked me up and down. "Now that's another story."

"Great. I guess we need to do some negotiating then."

"We do," he said, "but just remember Sitting Bull's wise observation, 'Sitting Bull live by three words: keep bow tight, keep arrow sharp, and no put money into show bidness.'"

"I never heard that before. Where does it come from?"

"It's from 'Annie Get Your Gun.' I played Sitting Bull in the first Theatre Under the Stars production way back in the late 50s."

"But *you* put money in—and you're still around. You must have done something right."

"It's a long story," he said. "I'll tell you about it sometime. Now I've got a lot to do. Why don't you go back home and think about some sort of agreement, then mail me your ideas. Maybe you can come down from Ottawa and we can meet when I come to Toronto next month." He resumed his scribbling as if this intrusion was a minor irritant to the efficient accomplishment of his day.

With that, we parted.

Six months of long-distance, protracted negotiations later I was back in the smoky art deco office for good, with Ben as my partner and mentor.

Ours was an unusual relationship, a partnership forged from the vagaries of fate rather than the certainties of sustained friendship. It was like an arranged marriage, groom meeting bride for the first time on their wedding day. Surprises waited. We were two distinctly different individuals.

Eighteen years my senior, Ben proved to be irascible and quick-tempered; he usually operated by the seat of his pants. I was naïve and more mellow; I subscribed to a studied approach to business. Needless to say, Ben was the senior partner and he was determined to teach me "street smarts."

The early lessons were tough.

* * *

Almost on my first day, Ben pulled me into his office and growled, "You should be out at all the gigs we book at least for the first six months until you get to know every act and what they can do." We probably had a hundred or more acts and performers that we worked with on a regular basis. This was going to occupy most of my evenings. Plus I wondered why.

He read my mind. "It's impossible to do a good job as an agent if you don't have a clue about what you're booking."

"That's reasonable."

"If you can't make it to see them, I want you to call the acts the next morning and see how their gig went," he added. "Oh, yeah, and when you go to see them, make sure you take their cheque."

"Wait a minute," I said. "Don't agencies represent the performers? I thought *they* paid *us* a commission."

"We do it a bit differently. We're more like a middleman. We take their fee and put our commission on top and bill our clients—companies, hotels, whoever. It's easier to get the money and it speeds up the process. Performers and clients are happier that way."

"OK, fair enough," I said, "but I thought it was good accounting practice to wait to pay your suppliers. Why do you do that? Doesn't it put a strain on your cash flow? You have to wait to be paid by your clients."

"Let me tell you a little story." He looked deadly serious as he leaned back in his oversized chair. "Have a seat." Something told me this was important.

"When I first came to Vancouver," he said, "I had a friend named Max. Besides acting, we both loved comedy and we put together a duo comedy act. We bounced our jokes off each other and just enjoyed the electricity between us. Got lots of great reaction from audiences. We did a lot of club dates and one night we played a stag at a golf club. Everyone was drunk. They started yelling anti-Semitic comments at us. Max and I looked at each other and walked offstage in the middle of the show. Remember, this wasn't that long after the war." He paused to let the image sink in. "We never did the comedy act again."

Having been a performer myself, I knew that the worst nightmare of anyone who loves being onstage was to be unappreciated, to be scorned. A racial slur was the ultimate in humiliation.

"And you know the worst of it?" he said. "The fellow who booked us was a newspaper salesman and he never even called us to ask how the show went. That's when the seed was planted to be a booking agent. When I finally became one, that was my first rule: make sure the performers are treated well."

"Sounds pretty smart," I said.

"Oh, and another thing. Most performers live from hand to mouth. They don't like you knowing it but they do. I've been there. They appreciate being paid promptly."

From then on, I always paid my acts immediately after their performances or I called them to check on how their shows went and mailed their cheques the next day. It paid off, too. I often received referrals to clients *from* my performers. One even resulted in a contract worth over eighty thousand dollars.

Reputation was and is everything for a small business, so treating suppliers—performers in our case—with respect went a long way to cementing that reputation.

Years after selling my company I was helping to produce a special Remembrance Day show for the local theatre where I volunteered, and I called up an old musician friend, Tom, whom we used to hire on a regular basis. He was to be the musical director. We were getting close to contract time and had one last meeting with him to go over songs and show flow. He seemed a bit preoccupied.

"Doug, I have to tell you. I've got an offer for another gig on the same night as this show. It's for a lot more money and none of the work and rehearsal time required for this one."

The show's director was with us. He looked crestfallen. "Gosh, that's too bad. We were really looking forward to working with you," he said.

"Don't worry," Tom said, "I'm not taking the other gig. I'm doing this one because it's for Doug."

* * *

Coming directly out of Canada's military as a senior officer into a job as a self-employed person in a small service business brought a load of conflicting beliefs and feelings. I was educated to be a leader, but as soon as I took off my uniform for the last time I was a servant. Ben didn't waste any time in reminding me of this fact.

I called it the humility factor. I no longer had any subordinates to do my bidding. Instead, every client was my boss. And it wasn't just a single contact person; every person who attended a conference or a dinner at which we had entertainment was a boss. It was difficult to get my head around this new reality.

Ben soon straightened me out at a large conference for which we were parading guests to dinner with a pipe band. We were both dressed in our "second skins," tuxedoes with our own company nametags. It was almost impossible to distinguish us from hotel catering staff.

"When the band parades through the reception area, you get over to those doors that lead down the hall to dinner and hold them open," he demanded gruffly. "We have to make it easy for the five hundred guests to get in."

What?? Flunkies do that, I thought. Or why not hotel staff?

"And don't forget to smile at everyone," he added, as he signalled the band to start playing.

Fifteen minutes of perma-smile later, I started to get the point.

Ben had been watching from the side of the hall as the parade unfolded, puffing on his cigarette—long before laws preventing such air pollution. He marched over to me and drove his point home. "Remember this. From now on, if you see a piece of décor out of place, or a person who's lost, or a performer who needs a glass of water, you fix the problem. Don't wait for anyone else to do it. You're part of a team."

A good portion of the time we spent at events was waiting in hotel ballrooms, usually after dinners, while acts strutted their stuff onstage. Within six months I truly felt I was a member of the "service team" in all the venues where we worked. In fact, I even tracked my progress. The two questions most asked of me were, "Where's the washroom?" and "Can we have more wine?"

I never let on I wasn't catering staff. I just made sure I knew the answers—and that I gave them with a smile.

* * *

"You have two jobs now," Ben said near the beginning. "You show up for work during the day, then you put on your tux and you work the shows at night. It's just part of having your own business."

And he wasn't kidding. My cushy, forty-hour-per-week government job was soon a distant memory as fifty- and sixty-hour weeks became the norm. I loved the entertainment business, so that didn't bother me at all, although the finer details of the civilian work ethic were a shock at first. Any hint of idle time was not part of this ethic.

One day I was joking on the phone with a performer I knew well.

Ben laid down the law. "I'm a nose-to-the-grindstone kind of guy," he said, as he put down his pen from a frantic marathon of letter writing. "When you're in the office, it's work time. Every minute counts. If conversations start going astray too much, it's time to end them. Your first priority should be to bring in new contracts, and after that to deal with the ones you already have. You can't make money pissing away the time with gossip."

I felt chastised for a minor lapse but realized that my income no longer dropped conveniently from publicly cultivated trees.

Our noses were usually well polished by that high-speed grindstone, but when I experienced a month without any substantial contracts, I began fretting. Because it was a quiet month, Ben and I actually did squeeze a few moments of leisure time into the tail end of a Friday. He opened his credenza and brandished a twelve-year-old Balvenie.

"For sipping on special occasions."

"I thought we didn't have any spare time."

"Today we do. We need to talk." He poured us each a couple of fingers. "L'chei-im."

"Cheers."

Then he settled back into his big chair with a cigarette in one hand and the whisky in the other. He looked out the window.

"OK, what do we need to talk about?" I asked.

"You look worried."

"Yeah, I am. I just want to make sure I can pay the mortgage. Don't you ever worry?"

He coughed the day's smoky cobwebs from his lungs. As usual, a gem of wisdom followed. "You have to understand the business," he said slowly.

"What have I missed?"

"One year will be up, one will be down. One month will be up, one will be down. In fact, we have regular months that are up and regular ones that are down."

"That helps a bit," I said, "but what if you have a string of bad months?"

"First of all, you put the money away from the good years—don't spend it all at once or pay yourself all of it. You might see one really great year in ten."

"Hmm, nice to know."

Ben spun around in his chair and faced me directly. He sipped the Scotch, preparing.

"Second, if you really like what you do and you keep that work ethic, there's a good—no, a *better* than good— chance that the business will come. Remember, it only takes one phone call. You've gotta have faith. Sit back and enjoy the ride."

"OK, I'll keep that in mind."

Five years after Ben retired, I had a banner year. Except for some employee bonuses, I socked the excess into the bank.

Three years later, I was audited by the provincial government. They claimed I owed them forty-eight thousand dollars in back sales taxes. I thought it was the end. It was a huge sum for a small business. I was distraught, but I dutifully paid the amount in instalments and laid off a couple of employees to keep the business going. I was determined not to let this ruin my company.

I launched an appeal, convinced I had done nothing wrong, and put my nose even closer to the grindstone.

Then I prayed and waited for that one phone call.

It was a tough time and we hobbled along, but no single saving call came. It was hard to enjoy what was proving to be a very bumpy ride on this stretch of road.

One year after the audit, two men in dark suits came to my office.

"Mr. Matthews, we're from the government."

Uh, oh!

"Come in. Have a seat," I said. My employees pretended not to notice what was going on.

"You've won your appeal." They let the words sink in.

I just stared, not totally comprehending.

"We apologize for any inconvenience. You will be receiving a cheque very shortly for the amount you've already paid."

The government actually apologized—and in front of witnesses!

As I recall, the sun shone particularly brightly that day.

The old showman would have been proud.

* * *

Like all businesses, we had a telephone answering machine. Whoever came in first in the morning played the messages back. Ben was usually first because he lived closer, but one day I made it in before him. There was one message. It was a husky female voice.

"You hunk of f… meat, I want to grab your big c… and r… it. I want to make you scream for more…"

I listened with my mouth agape as various other vivid descriptions of what this faceless woman wanted to do to at least one of us spewed out of the machine. The last I looked we didn't represent any porn stars, nor were any of our clients so inclined. What was this all about?

When Ben arrived, I played it back for him. He looked unruffled.

"Yeah, we get quite a few of those. You never hear them because I erase them," he said.

"So what's the story?"

"If you notice in the Yellow Pages, Entertainment Agencies come pretty close to Escort Agencies."

"So?"

"So some of the dumb-asses who call for escorts think we do the same thing. I just ignore them."

"Maybe we can help to lessen the effect," I said.

"And how do you plan to do that?"

"Well, think about it. The escort agencies use giant Yellow Page ads. They must get a lot of business from them. Why don't we try the same thing? Besides, none of our competitors are doing it. We would stand out, maybe attract more people. If we spell out what we do, the escort looky-loos might understand that we don't provide hookers."

"I don't think so. It's too expensive."

It took a couple of more months and a few more obscene calls before Ben was convinced. Our larger ad ran in the next instalment of the Yellow Pages and the obscene calls stopped. We even managed to more than pay for the ad with increased business.

The story was similar with a fax machine. I noticed that the fax was starting to be the norm in transmitting documents rather than regular mail. I tried to convince Ben.

"Think about how much sooner we could get our proposals sent out and contracts signed if we used a fax," I said, trying my best to present a logical argument.

"No, it's too expensive. We don't need it."

I persisted, every few days throwing in my argument for a fax. Finally, he relented. Business became more efficient. Contracts were flying to and from clients. Proposals were going out quicker and answers coming back faster. We were really on a roll. Four years into our partnership, I started to make the case for computers. I hit a brick wall.

"Don't want 'em, don't need 'em, never will," said Ben.

It was about then that he appeared to be increasingly stressed and soon called it quits from the business.

I went on to embrace computers and cell phones and all things technologically modern. I thought I had to keep up. After all, business was accelerating. E-mails came in asking us for proposals by the next day. Contracts were turned around instantly. Phone calls were endless. Holidays were too short. Taking a couple of hours for a leisurely business lunch with a potential client was a thing of the past.

Within ten years I too was starting to feel more stressed—much more than I ever had been when I first joined the company. It was then that I realized that in his profound wisdom, Ben had seen the future.

Chapter Three

Shanks

One of my tasks in our company was to mine talent. As a result, I spent many an evening cruising smoky bars and clubs auditioning bands and assorted weird acts. Near the beginning, a place in the Vancouver suburb of Maple Ridge brought back a collection of dusty memories from years before when I lived in Alberta.

* * *

The call came on a late November evening, just after dinner. It was Guitar God.

"Doogie, we got it!" he said.

"Got what?"

"The gig, man, the gig at Shanks. End of next week. Thursday, Friday, Saturday nights."

"Nice goin', Larry. What's the pay?"

"Six hundred bucks."

"Wow, not bad. That's per night, right?"

"Uh, no, all three nights."

"Per person?" I sensed exploitation.

"No again. Total, but they said they'd raise it if we did well and came back for another weekend."

"Shit, good thing we all have day jobs and like music."

"Hey, look at it this way, Doogie. We're gonna get known better and then we'll get more gigs out of this one. It's a stepping stone."

"OK, OK. It should be a gas, anyway. Rehearsal this weekend, same time?"

"Yeah. We have to be off-book," he said, reminding me that music onstage didn't cut it. "Practise up, buddy. See you then."

This call set in motion several things. First, I had to spend all my non-working hours over the next week and a half memorizing music. Second, Guitar God was now to be recognized as our official leader since he had managed to get us the most work. Third, visions of rock stardom began to dance in our heads, along with all the beguiling temptations those visions held.

In reality, "we" were an odd collection of four guys and one girl moonlighting as 80s weekend rock stars. Odd because most of us were in the military at Canadian Forces Base Cold Lake, Alberta, and had no hope of becoming rock stars—our hair was just too short and, well, talent questionable. The odd man out, Tooth Fairy, was a longhaired air force brat right out of high school. He played bass—really well. Come to think of it, he was the only one destined for anything close to stardom. The name—oh yeah, it came from his last baby molar he'd hung like a medal around his neck. Kids do the strangest things.

Newf was the drummer. The first time we met he said, "Jaysus, bye, you bin around since Christ was a cowboy." It was pretty obvious what his nickname was going to be, and yes, he saw in me the wisdom of age. I was thirty-six.

Pipes was the singer, our token female—young, single, good curb appeal for the bars.

We called ourselves "Touch of Class" and near the beginning of our existence had considered the more controversial "Touch of Ass" but thought better of it. Too much temptation to sample one of Pipes' best attributes.

Anyway, two weeks rolled around way too fast, and we were soon rolling the five kilometres to town and our first multi-day gig.

Alberta chic meets broken 50s neon. That was one of the kinder descriptions of the main entrance to the Grand Cold Lake Hotel in 1983, otherwise known as Shanks. A three-storey red brick façade outlined by wooden beams rendered it a solid, upstanding citizen next to the sleazier stucco neighbours that had sprung up around it in the boom years of the 50s.

Double doors of glass and wood with huge brass handles were topped by a twenty-foot-long green sign with the hotel's name majestically painted in red. Apart from the easy association with a perennial Christmas tree sale, the sign looked almost professional during the day. Unfortunately, at night, the name was outlined in red neon and, neon being a light source of low popularity in northeastern Alberta since the 50s, it was never kept in good operating condition. Hence, the arriving visitor was greeted by "…an…ol…ake…otel" if it was dark, leaving him wondering just how comfortable his stay might indeed be.

But the hotel made its income from the bar, not the rooms. The bar was just inside to the left, through another dented wooden door. Once across this dynamic threshold, the visitor—or rather patron—was thrust into the sensual mélange of the all-Canadian beer parlour. Thirty years' worth of perfumed memories lay on the floor in a thick black and gold shag pile.

On this particular evening, a Thursday, we parked around back in the alley. Then we all went in together to check out the setup before unloading our gear.

It was 8:15. A handful of scruffy patrons in assorted ball caps ignored us—except when Pipes walked in at the end. Then the eyes turned. There was promise in the air.

We approached the bartender, a fat guy with long sideburns.

"We're the band for this weekend," Guitar God said. "Any special rules about setting up or playing?"

"Yeah. That's the stage," he said, pointing to a tiny patch of dirty linoleum about thirty feet to his right. "Try to fit everything onto it." We all cringed at once. It looked big enough to accommodate a couple of amps at best.

"You got power over there?" Guitar God asked. The corner of the room was pitch black.

"Two sockets in the wall. Don't overload them or the whole bar loses power and then the fights start," Sideburns said.

"What about breaks and drinks?" Newf said, concerned that a dry gig was never a good gig.

"Music starts at 9:00 and last call's at 12:30. You can take fifteen minutes every hour. Beer's the same price as for regular customers."

"You're a prince, bye. Tanks for that," Newf said. The wheels turned in Sideburns's head as he tried to place the accent.

Newf read his mind. "Yeah, it's a Newfie accent. Don't be lookin' so strange at me, now. I'll be pullin' your chain lots while we're here." He winked as we turned to load in.

Rock and roll in the 80s was all about big gear. Guitars with two necks, keyboardists surrounded by mountains of keyboards that resembled the bridge on the Enterprise, and huge, two-hundred-pound amps. Any musician who played something electronic, which was pretty well everyone, had to have a huge amp. I felt inadequate with a single synthesizer. The saving grace was that I had the biggest and heaviest amp of any of us. As I groaned, swore, and willed it into place beside the others at the back of the "stage," my mind flew back to happier times when all a piano player had to do was show up and sit down at the house piano. No gear. Zip. No heavy lifting. No hernias. Of course there was the time when I played on a relic with cracked keys and blood all over them. On second thought, maybe my own keyboard and amp wasn't such a bad idea.

But that was then, this was now. We had set up a veritable wall of sound behind us. The "stage" was so small, in fact, that the wall was touching our butts as we played. Pipes could venture a little farther out since she was connected only by a long, umbilical mic cord to the rest of us. Our setup was pretty simple. She and the other singers—Guitar God and Tooth Fairy—had mics through the PA. Otherwise, all sound came from the wall of amps.

Four modest lights pierced the bar's smoky atmosphere and announced where we were. Nobody knew much about colour combinations in those days, and so we didn't care that we looked green, only that we had light.

That first night, things were quiet. By the last set, after a few beers, we laid hard into some Eagles' songs and that got half the room up dancing. Mostly, though, everyone ignored us. The Indians and oil patch crowd kept talking to themselves. Another group of regulars, the farmers, wanted more country and shouted a few unintelligible comments. The last group, the air force, played drinking games and hogged the pool tables. We didn't even have to crank up the volume. For a bar band, that was a bad sign.

After we finished, Tooth Fairy said, "We shoulda been louder."

"Maybe more rock and less Anne Murray tomorrow night," I said.

Guitar God said it was early yet. "Let's wait for tomorrow and see what happens."

Pipes mumbled something about being fondled at the bar before the last set.

Newf summed up the general consensus. "These goofs don't know a good band when dey see one. We're the best ting to hit here in years."

Nevertheless, we left at 1:00 a.m. a little disheartened, wondering if we were going to manage to stay even until Saturday.

Since our gear was already there, our three-car convoy arrived at 8:45 the next night and we ambled in through the back door just behind the stage. Inside, we couldn't believe our eyes.

"Will ya look at that, boys? Dey love us," Newf said.

"Holy shit!" Tooth Fairy said.

"I'm nervous. I gotta pee," Pipes said.

The room was awash in a sea of coloured ball caps, not a seat to be found. Farmers, Indians, oil workers, military—all smoking, laughing, swearing excitedly. The prairie heartland at its most gregarious. At home. Here in our bar. Waiting for us. Barmaids with heavy mascara and short black skirts squeezed between the crowded tables.

I turned my gear on, waited for the hum of the amp, then headed to the bar for a couple of warm-up beers. I knew about that knife-edge point—too few and you kept the stage fright, too many and you fell over the edge into sloppy playing. Two were my limit—at least to begin.

"You guys gotta get started," Sideburns said, his voice a little higher pitched than last night. He was obviously stressed. "These folks are gettin' antsy."

"Yeah, for sure. This is great. They're here to see us, right?" I said.

"Are you kidding? The power went out in a couple of hangars on the base late this afternoon. Most of them have been sitting here for over four hours. Nothin' else to do. As for the rest of them, it's payday."

I didn't have the heart to tell Guitar God or the others.

We opened with the usual Anne Murray. Not much action on the dance floor.

Pipes got into "Hit Me with Your Best Shot" by Pat Benatar and a lot of the oil patchers moved onto the floor, their girlfriends in tow. Blonde hair and ball caps began bobbing up and down in synchronous euphoria.

Guitar God said something like, "I think we got the formula," from the far side of the stage and signalled to follow the rock set list. He moved us into Fleetwood Mac's "Don't Stop." All the air force guys with short hair and their big-boobed girls leapt up. Next came some country rock from Alabama. That brought the Indians and farmers out of their fish stories and divorce woes. The room exploded. From then on, the dance floor was full.

By the end of the first set, forty minutes later, we were all sweating and smiling. Happy B.O. and assorted colognes—some enticing and some downright obnoxious—were added to the room's sensual appeal. The barmaids went nuts refilling beer orders at the tables. Pipes occupied herself trying to convince a forty-five-year-old, cigar-wielding fighter-jet jock that she was not for sale. Nope, not even for a free drink or a ride in his "machine." Newf, Guitar God, Tooth Fairy, and I hastened to the bar to replenish our lost sweat in the most meaningful way.

"Not bad," Sideburns said.

"Not bad?" Newf said. "We were frickin' awesome, bye."

"You keep that floor full for three more sets and my beer flowing and you'll be here again." Sideburns nodded, almost convincingly.

"I told ya," Guitar God said, proud of himself.

"You are mighty, indeed, oh wise leader," Tooth Fairy said. We all bowed to Guitar God.

After a few swills I went to the washroom while the others rescued Pipes and continued to pat themselves heavily on the back. It was there that I noticed things might go sideways in the not-too-distant future. This time, I didn't keep it secret.

"Don't turn your backs on anyone in the washroom," I volunteered as I returned to the band's table.

"Why? What's goin' on?" Guitar God said.

"Were ya propositioned, my son?" Newf grinned.

"Nah, nothing like that," I said. "Only blood smeared all over the walls and mirrors."

"Lard Jaysus, cowboys and Indians all over again," Newf said.

"Well, there's lots of them here," Tooth Fairy said.

"I haven't seen any fights, yet," Pipes said, "only a couple of guys who keep staring at me and arguing."

"They're probably bettin' how many beers it'll take till you look good," Newf said. "I'd say about eight. How about you guys?"

"Ah, give her some credit, man. She's a six," Tooth Fairy said.

"Hey, shut up, you dirt bags," Pipes said. "What about the blood?"

Guitar God played it safe. "Well, if we don't give 'em some music soon, they're gonna look to fight *us*, then it'll be *our* blood." He stood up and motioned to the stage. "Let's just hope nothin' happens."

The next couple of sets were like the first, frenetic. We kept a lookout for fights but the only thing that flew in the room were crude jokes, not punches, although some rather odd relationships seemed to be developing.

A visiting squadron of fighter jocks—the same group that had produced Pipes's admirer—was hell-bent on partying like there was no tomorrow, trading spit with some local Lolitas, most likely nurses from the air force base. The farmers and oil workers tried to out-shout themselves requesting songs. A few who had succumbed to the long night rested their heads on the beery tables or each other's shoulders.

Of course, as part of our sets, like a good bar band, we had to throw in the occasional slow song if for no other reason than to give the house a chance to sell more drinks. In the middle of the third set, I noticed a couple on the floor during "Angel of the Morning" by Juice Newton. He was the Canadian version of Paul Bunyan, topping at near six feet four inches and closing in on two hundred eighty pounds. A blue ball cap, red-checkered shirt, long hair, and beard completed the comparison. She was a petite Indian princess in white leather with matching white boots. She stood all of five feet one inch and the boots might have given her an extra inch. They were clearly passionate about each other, locked in an embrace and barely moving. She had her arms around his ample torso—well, halfway around—her head pressed into his belly. He hunched over her like a grizzly about to devour his prey. It was a funny scene but heartwarming at the same time. Back at their table they continued to grope and cling. We played through the set and thought no more about it.

During our last break for sweat replacement, we happened to mention the blood in the washroom to Sideburns.

"Oh, that," he said. "It's probably Tommy McLean." Sideburns pointed to a slight kid a few tables away. He looked barely twenty. Tommy smirked toothlessly back at Sideburns. "He's a little nuts. He often gets nosebleeds and likes to smear it on walls. He thinks it's a joke."

"Geez, man, it looks like Freddie Krueger visited," Newf said.

"Yeah, it's pretty gross. Can't you do something about it?" said Tooth Fairy.

"Hey, Tommy," Sideburns shouted, "go clean up your mess or you're cut off."

Tommy sauntered over, now unsmiling, picked up a huge wet towel that Sideburns handed him, and dutifully retreated to the confines of the horror house to mop up.

"And don't miss any spots," Sideburns shouted after him. Tommy threw his arms up and plodded on.

Set number four was a barnburner. All rock. We started with a Journey song. Hell, nobody played Journey. It was just too hard. But Guitar God had the licks, so we tackled it and the crowd loved it. Somewhere in the middle of the set, Tooth Fairy and Guitar God decided they couldn't hear the rest of us over the din. Guitar God gave the signal.

"Crank 'er!" I saw his lips move, but I couldn't hear what came out. I knew what he meant, though. It was a good sign. My amp shrieked into overdrive.

The rest of the night was ear-splitting pandemonium. During Van Halen's "Jump"—the song that gave me instant respect for Eddie as a keyboard player—the room was reverberating at a hundred twenty beats per, like a giant heart. The whole building was moving. It felt like we were inside some alien organism doing aerobics. Even Paul Bunyan and his Indian princess were jumping up and down, hair flying in every direction.

At the end of the set at 1:00 a.m., the patrons—at least those still standing—gave us a raucous cheer.

Pipes, whose voice was pretty well shot, whispered huskily, "Awesome gig, you guys. This was fun, even though I got groped again."

"Well, what did ya expect?" Tooth Fairy said. "They've all had more than six beer."

"Eight," Newf said.

"Boys, boys. Have a heart. You did us proud, Pipes," I said.

"Good going everyone, and get this." Guitar God was setting us up, I was sure. "Sideburns says we can come back in two weeks for another weekend."

"You mean he's the owner?" I said.

"Lard Jaysus, I shoulda treated him with more respect," Newf said.

The room continued to involuntarily convulse with post-orgasmic conversations and final goodbyes. Suddenly in the middle of the dance floor there was a blur of white leather and red tartan. A heated conversation quickly turned into a barrage of swearing and shouts as Paul Bunyan and the Indian princess went at it. She swung a couple of wild punches at his gut. He grabbed her arm and then they were down on the floor rolling around. In one of the strangest fighting manoeuvres I had ever seen, he grabbed one of her white leather boots off a foot, took a bite out of it, then flung it across the room. It landed with a thunk on a table, breaking four or five half-empty beer glasses.

The princess lost it. "You fucking asshole. I thought you liked me and now you've ruined my boot and my evening. You're a goddamn turd." She jumped astride his belly and proceeded to pound his face with her small fists. He tried in vain to protect himself from the storm of blows. After a dozen or so, she landed a haymaker and he was out.

Newf said, "Ain't love grand?"

"Aw, and they made such a cute couple," Pipes said.

"Nice clientele," Tooth Fairy said.

"Always some kind of action at Shanks," Guitar God said.

Sideburns jumped in at that moment and told her to take it outside. He dragged Paul Bunyan to the back door. The princess limped out behind him, mumbling every insult she could conjure up.

We all followed. In the alley, the December cold had revived Paul Bunyan and the two of them were rolling around in a light dusting of snow, still cursing each other.

As we got in our cars to leave, I said to Guitar God, "By the way, man, nobody ever told me why they call this place Shanks."

"You mean you don't know?" he said. "It's the name on the toilets."

"That fits," I said.

We ended up being the house band for the next year.

Chapter Four

Gremlins

As American motivational speaker and author Denis Waitley writes, "Expect the best, plan for the worst, and prepare to be surprised."

Planning for every eventuality was second nature to us. In the world of special event entertainment there was only one chance to get it right. Seldom was there any time for more than a short rehearsal to test sound systems, blocking onstage, or the movement of performers to and from green rooms. Try to avoid them though we did, gremlins seemed to invade our lives at the most inopportune and unexpected times.

* * *

One of our best clients was an organization that held an annual awards banquet for the city's business community. Each year they created a themed event with food, decorations, and entertainment centered on the theme.

In 1991, we celebrated the seven-hundredth anniversary of the founding of Switzerland. We had alpine horns, yodellers, chocolate, and everything Swiss that we could think of. Our client invited the Swiss ambassador and the lieutenant-governor of our province. Of course, when such dignitaries are present, some protocol is involved.

One such item of protocol was the strict observance of the order of entry into the dining room and the playing of appropriate national anthems. While the VIPs entered, all in attendance stood out of respect. Once the lieutenant-governor reached his seat, we were to immediately play a piece of music entitled the Vice Regal Salute, which consisted of the first six bars of "God Save the Queen" immediately followed by the first four and last four bars of "O Canada." This was all recorded, so it was easy. For the Swiss event, we were also required to play the Swiss national anthem.

At an organizing committee meeting a few weeks before the event, one of the Swiss representatives asked me if I needed a CD copy of the Swiss anthem. I said no thanks as I had already visited a music store and purchased the latest CD version of "Anthems of the World," on which was that very anthem. Now, that was initiative, I figured. It should make me look good to my client.

The parade to dinner went smoothly. All the dignitaries arrived in the right order and we proceeded into the dining room. I was on intercom to my audio engineer so I could cue him at the appropriate moment. The Vice Regal Salute was bang on. Then came the Swiss anthem. As it played, I noticed that all the guests were laughing. This was not good. It had the exact same melody as "God Save the Queen," and, since it was an instrumental version, I realized they thought I was playing the wrong anthem. Just shows their ignorance, I thought. The joke's on them. Wait till they find out.

Then the MC explained what had happened.

"In fact," he said to all assembled, "the *old* Swiss anthem was indeed the same melody as 'God Save the Queen,' but it was replaced recently by a newer song that could not be mistaken. Our apologies, Mr. Ambassador."

Fortunately, the guests were all looking at him. They didn't notice my face turning scarlet.

* * *

For about a fifteen-year period during initial growth of the special events industry, decorative sculptures constructed purely of balloons were all the rage. Some of these were massive, as large as forty or fifty feet high or long. There were even competitions for the most creative.

We used such a sculpture for a conference dinner at a local university. It was a twenty-foot-wide by ten-foot-high wall of balloons, which, on cue, would explode, instantly revealing the dance band waiting behind it. It was a special effect intended to be a perfect segue from the dinner and formal presentations to the dance portion of the evening.

The evening was beautiful. The warm, late-June sunlight streamed through the floor-to-ceiling windows. Guests were in a gregarious, jovial mood. Our balloon wall looked spectacular. The balloon experts had even created the client's logo pattern as part of the wall. All we had to do was get through the dinner and surreptitiously place the band behind the wall while everyone's attention was focused on speeches later in the evening.

However, there were other plans afoot.

Just as dinner was underway, we heard an explosion. Someone must have accidentally burst a balloon, I thought. A minute later, there was another one … and another … and another.

Now this was truly worrisome. Too many to be a coincidence.

In short order, over half the wall exploded—completely without human intervention. Ten minutes later, it was a scene of total carnage. The wire support structure resembled a dead monster's skeleton, ragged pieces of balloons hanging from it like broken flesh in a myriad of colours.

Most of us remember the first time we burned a dry leaf using a magnifying glass, perhaps our first encounter with the simple yet awesome power of the sun. Our balloon wall was like that leaf, the recipient of the sun's power beaming through the windows.

Mother Nature had trumped technology.

* * *

It was the middle of a keynote address to a major conference about human interaction and training. Several of the five hundred audience members had already begun to doze off as the PowerPoint slides rolled on. The speaker was nearing a critical juncture in his speech. It was deadly serious.

I was at the back of the room sipping coffee and talking to someone. I had ceased paying attention to the presentation, as all I had to do was ensure that the audio-visual components functioned properly, which included the audio, lighting, and projector systems. Everything appeared to be well under control, that is until a collective guffaw arose from the suddenly wide-awake audience.

The speaker stopped mid-sentence. He looked stunned.

"Was that what I think it was?" he asked the audience as he glanced over his shoulder at the screen behind him.

Amidst the snickers I heard, "Yup." "It was." "Oops." "That was weird."

Feeling a little dumb, I asked, "What happened?" to a woman in the last row of seats.

"You mean you didn't see that?" she answered. "A silhouette of a nude dancer cartwheeled across the screen just as the speaker was going to give us the main message. It was hilarious. A bit of bad timing, though. Someone's going to be in trouble."

I glanced up and realized that someone was me.

Up until that time, I had only known my client as an easygoing, affable woman. Apparently she had another side, and that side was clearly broadcast by the expression of rage on her face. Within seconds she was at the control desk.

"What the hell was that?" she asked. "It was inexcusable." Her face was red and she was shaking. This didn't look good.

My video technician, who controlled the PowerPoint projection, looked sheepish. "Sorry, I pushed the wrong button." At least he was smart enough to own up to it, since he was the only one at the controls. I knew I should have been watching him more closely.

My client's gaze drilled through me. "You make bloody sure that doesn't happen again. I don't want any more glitches."

By now the humour of what had happened struck me and I had trouble stifling a giggle as I responded, "We will. No problem." The irony of the blunder was that it might very well cement the speaker's message in the audience's memory better than anything could, but I didn't offer that viewpoint to my client.

A couple of minutes later, I retreated to a distant corner and laughed out loud. The juxtaposition of the serious presentation with the crazy screen wipe just wouldn't leave my mind. Someone, though—and probably something— had to be sacrificed.

I never hired the video technician again. But, being a businessman and wanting to *stay* in business, I offered my client a substantial discount and an apology. Her response was unusual.

"Tell you what," she said. "Why don't you just bill us for the entire amount and then give your discount to our charity?"

"Great idea." I'd never thought of that as a way out. "I will."

A week later I received an accolade letter and a nice jacket with the charity's logo on it. Apparently, they liked my "proactive mindset."

I learned a lesson about supervision—and how easy it is for technology to turn against you—but I still chuckle about the screen wipe.

* * *

There is no single job in today's entertainment and special event world that is more fraught with peril and stress than the position of technical director. Also known as a "show caller," this is the person who literally makes everything happen when it's supposed to—and sometimes even when it's not. This is the general leading his or her troops into the valley of death, or perhaps the valley of rapturous joy, as the case may be, depending on the outcome of the event. I was that person on numerous occasions.

This was an annual awards night with lots of media coverage and hundreds of VIP guests. The main part of the event occurred after dinner and it was all on the stage.

I knew it was going to be a tough night when the illuminated stage backdrop appeared to shake. I glanced up. The lights hanging from the main truss on the ceiling were bouncing up and down. Strange. I didn't feel an earthquake. I hoped the trussing was safe. If it fell, half the audience would be injured or killed.

"What's going on?" I asked my lighting director.

"No idea. Let me check." I figured he was going to check the trussing supports.

Five minutes later he returned. "There's a rock band in the ballroom above us. It could be like this all night," he said. "They're shaking the floor—our ceiling."

"Too bad the hotel conveniently forgot to warn us about this." I was miffed that after all our planning and dialogue with the hotel, this happened. "Too late to worry about it now."

The shaking continued all during the dinner. It stopped just before the awards were to begin. Ah, a reprieve. Maybe it won't be so bad after all, I thought.

Then it was time for the awards. Just as with the Oscars, there were speeches by VIPs, awards introductions given by presenters, presentation of the actual award, and a speech by the recipient. The whole show would probably take about three hours. I had over forty pages of script and cues to call to ensure it went off smoothly. I was on the first page.

Voiceover: "Now please welcome the president of the academy, Mr. W. D.!" The recorded voiceover was loud and clear. Mr. D. walked onstage to the lectern. He looked proud and happy to be there.

Mr. D.'s mouth moved but nothing came out.

"Shit, shit, shit! What's happening?" I screamed to the audio engineer over the intercom. "Turn up the volume."

He did. The feedback squeal told us the speakers were not happy. "It all worked fine in rehearsal," he said, his voice rising in a question. He looked flabbergasted, poring over the myriad buttons and sliders that comprised the large audio console.

I don't think he has a clue, I realized. How did we get this guy?

"Can you find a wireless?" I asked him.

"One's coming from backstage." As he said this, a stage manager ran out to Mr. D.

Mr. D. had been patient. He still had a glimmer of a fake smile. He raised the wireless microphone to his lips. Again they moved but no sound emerged.

Oh, boy, now we're in serious trouble. I mentally tried to find a reason to make an extended search for a lost pencil under the table.

"We've got another one," the audio engineer said.

"Get it!" I yelled into the intercom.

By now, Mr. D.'s glow had turned to gloom. The pregnant pause had given birth to extended audience conversation.

Mr. D. pressed on when the second wireless microphone arrived. My engineer managed to eke out enough volume this time that Mr. D. finished his speech while the audience barely listened.

We replaced the lectern microphones and the rest of the event proceeded uneventfully.

As it turned out, we analysed that the microphones—at least the wireless ones—had been subjected to radio frequency interference from the communication systems of nearby ships and planes. Well, it made for a good excuse. I knew that human systems were the main cause.

My hair turned a few shades greyer during those long silent minutes. I would not have wanted to test my blood pressure.

* * *

Because we worked mainly in hotels and conference centres, and because our job entailed moving performers to and from green rooms out of sight of audiences, we became acquainted with all the back hallways, kitchens, and stairs of these venues. We could get just about anywhere without being seen. Most venue staff recognized us by sight and let us do this unchallenged.

One of the hotels where we worked was a consistent winner of the American Automobile Association Five Diamond Award. That was the highest recognition a hotel could be given for superlative hospitality. We regularly received referrals from this hotel and knew it like the back of our hand.

A very exclusive group requested a show with two pianists playing back-to-back grand pianos in the ballroom of this hotel for a stylish dinner party. One of the pianists was to be attired in a white tux and playing a black piano, the other in a black tux and playing a white piano. I assigned the job to a new producer, Eric.

"Now remember," I said, "this is an important client who was referred by the hotel. You need to ensure that the show is going well, so you'll have to look in on them once or twice during the time they're playing. I've shown you the way to get around the back stairs."

"No problem," he said.

The next day, I asked Eric how the show went.

"Not bad." His voice was hesitant. "I got them started OK, but when I went to check on them an hour later like you said, I couldn't get into the room. The back door from the stairwell had been locked."

"That's not critical, as long as they started on time. They're pretty experienced musicians. I'll call the hotel to see how things went."

No sooner had I uttered the words than the phone rang. It was the hotel manager. Timely, I thought.

"Nice to hear from you, Mr. P. I was just thinking about you. How did the show go last night?" I asked.

"Are you kidding me? You're never going to work in this hotel again. You've received lots of referrals from us, but that's it. No more!" He slammed the phone down.

I turned to Eric. He had a sheepish "I've been discovered" look on his face.

"OK, what *really* happened?"

"Well, I got them started OK. Then I asked Jerry, the catering manager, to leave the doors to the ballroom unlocked so I could come back unnoticed an hour later to check on the show. He told me he would do it."

"So far, so good," I said. "Then what?"

"When I came back up the stairs the door was locked. I was kinda pissed, so I went all the way down to the next floor and came back up to the front of the ballroom but the security guys wouldn't let me in. I was pretty upset."

"And then?"

"I went back to the kitchen and found Jerry." Eric was reluctant to say any more. His face turned red.

"And?"

"And, uh, I slugged him," he said, his voice almost a whisper.

"You what!?"

"I hit him."

"Jesus, you don't do that to people who give us business. Hell, you shouldn't do that to anyone. That's not how you solve problems."

"I know. I'm sorry."

"Sorry's not good enough. You've just cost us thousands of dollars worth of business."

He was gone that day.

It took over ten years to repair our relationship with the hotel—and all because of a self-locking door.

* * *

I had done a few events in our city's domed stadium, but this one-hundredth anniversary celebration used only half the stadium. Because of this, my client wanted to block the other half off from view. I offered several options, the first being to hang drape from the ceiling of the stadium. But because the stadium was some one hundred feet in height, this would have been exorbitantly expensive, though it would have completely obscured the half of the stadium not in use. The second option was to hang twenty-foot-high velour drapes from sturdy *Genie super towers*, heavy-duty metal towers capable of supporting up to eight hundred pounds—not quite as expensive as the first option but not cheap. The third option was a series of ground-supported poles that would hold only twelve-foot-high velour drape and would be anchored with heavy sandbags. This was the cheapest option. My client chose the cheapest.

We set up the drapes so that they formed a barrier across the stadium field. The main stage backed onto this drape line but also had its own twenty-foot-high, black-drape backdrop anchored by the larger towers. Once complete, the entire setup looked clean and professional.

The first event of the day was a lengthy graduation ceremony. The afternoon was quite hot and the stadium had a white tension-fabric ceiling that absorbed the sunlight. At about 3:00 p.m., the whole building was beginning to seriously heat up. Unfortunately, it had no air conditioning. The only other option was a fan system that kept the air circulating throughout the stadium.

Now, I'm a person who loves the heat, so I found it just comfy. Apparently, most of the other five or six thousand attendees did not. I started receiving calls from my stage managers over the intercom.

"Doug, it's getting pretty hot in here. Is there anything we can do? Everyone's complaining."

"Sorry," I replied, "there's no air conditioning."

"What about the fan system? There doesn't seem to be any air circulation?"

"Let me check."

I radioed the stadium manager on duty. "Is it possible to turn on the fan system?"

"Sure, no problem, but it will take a few minutes to cool.

"OK, do it," I told her.

I waited patiently in front of the stage watching the ceremony. Suddenly, a wave-like cheer peeled around the audience seated in the rows of seats overlooking us as I felt the first "breeze" hit my face. I walked to the side of the stage in time to see the drape line collapsing like a row of dominoes across the stadium floor as the tsunami of air brought its cooling effect to the overheated masses.

"Holy shit!" I said over the intercom. "Nobody told me it would be *that* strong." With any fan system, one expects a gentle breeze wafting over the crowd and cooling them. In a sixty-thousand-seat stadium with a roof a hundred feet high, the air from fans does not waft. It blows with gale force as soon as it is turned on. The stadium manager had neglected to tell me that ahead of time.

The force of air combined with the weight of the drapes had brought all the drapes crashing to the floor amidst a twisted mess of metal supports. Fortunately, the stage drapery remained standing.

"Well, I guess that's what happens when you choose the cheap option. Sorry about mangling the supports. Can we get that all cleaned up?" I asked my lighting contractor who had supplied the drape and supports.

"We'll do our best," he said.

Within about half an hour his techs had taken away all signs of wind damage.

The graduation ceremony continued as if nothing had happened. My clients were onstage during the big blow and never made any mention of the drape collapse. They probably realized there was nothing to be gained by regretting the cheap option.

* * *

More and more events today rely on digital technology rather than what we used to call "analog" technology—the kind that required hundreds of dials and sliders. In many ways, the "one button with multiple uses concept" is a huge benefit to the efficient setup and execution of entertainment shows. There are, however, some disadvantages.

I was waiting backstage with Canadian country music star Michelle Wright as a spitfire auctioneer rambled through a long list of items, getting the audience pumped. Michelle was up after him.

Out front, my own audio engineer, Chris, was assisting Michelle's personal engineer, Danny, in getting ready for the show. Danny had brought in a very compact digital mixing console. I had heard the two of them talking about it earlier during a rehearsal.

Whereas the old fashioned analog one Chris used was about six feet wide, Danny proudly boasted about the extensive capabilities of his new two-foot-wide board.

"It can pre-record all the settings for the show. All I have to do is plug it in and the show's ready to go—virtually no rehearsal. It's been with us for this whole tour with Michelle, all over North America. Absolutely no problems."

Chris looked envious.

Danny continued, almost rubbing it in. "Everything can be recorded on a disk and I just insert it into the board. I carry around a separate disk for each different arena we play in."

Because of the "wonder board," the rehearsal was over in less than an hour, much more efficient that the normal two hours or more.

As I watched the auctioneer ramble on, I received an excited call from Chris over the intercom.

"Doug, we have to delay the show start as long as possible."

"Why? What happened?"

"We just had a power surge and it fried all the settings for Michelle's show that were on the disk. Danny has to re-program the entire show into his board."

"Crap. How long will that take?"

"Dunno. Could be half an hour."

"Well, I don't think we have that long, maybe ten minutes at best. I'll try to get the auction stretched out a bit. Keep me posted."

I looked over at Michelle. Her long, dark hair outlined her appealing features. She smiled and shifted from one foot to the other. I had to say something to her. I knew how performers hated waiting.

But not the whole truth. I liked her smile too much.

"Uh, Michelle, we're going to be a bit longer before show start. There are more auction items than we first thought."

"OK, no problem," she said. She was more patient than many others I knew.

I asked the auctioneer to extend and then spent the next minutes worrying whether he would run out of things to auction before the audio was ready. After seven or eight minutes, I could sense that keeping the auction going any longer would kill the show. The audience was getting impatient. We had to go.

"We need to start in two minutes," I signalled to Chris. "Is Michelle's show ready?"

A long, silent pause.

"No, Danny says it will take way too long to get all the cues back into the board. He's going to run it live."

I knew what this meant. Danny would have to monitor all the board settings continuously and use the first minutes of the show to set absolutely every single level on the board from scratch—the same thing that was normally done in the course of a two-hour rehearsal on an analog board. The likelihood of tremendous sound problems was very high, screaming feedback being one of the worst.

I cued Michelle. She had no idea what had happened, and I didn't tell her.

Unbelievably, other than a few motions from her to Danny to change monitor levels, the show was flawless—at least from my viewpoint. No question they were pros.

The client loved the show and never knew about the power surge and audio panic that had occurred. We were lucky.

Afterwards, I went back out front and talked to Chris, who had basically witnessed an hour of intense panic as his companion in the audio world fought to control Michelle's show. He had a big grin as he whispered in my ear, "I'm kinda glad I still have the old stuff. It's reliable as hell."

Danny departed with a brief thanks and goodbye. He never said another word about his new digital board.
From then on I viewed new technology with trepidatious optimism—and a healthy respect for the tried and true.

Chapter Five

Alberta Crud

Ben and I regularly brainstormed to find ideas for entertainment at events. On one occasion, we were looking for some new after-dinner activities. A light again illuminated my past life.

"What about crud?" I said.

"What the hell is crud?"

"You've never heard of the all-Canadian game?" Perhaps I'd pushed the astonishment factor too far. Groucho's eyebrows rose in scorn. He butted out a cigarette.

"I'm sure you're about to enlighten me."

I explained the rules as memories of my first encounter flooded back.

* * *

As it did every year, the late November prairie cold and snow had driven activities inside at the Officers' Mess of Canadian Forces Base Cold Lake, Alberta. It was early evening on Saturday, November 30, 1968, Grey Cup day. That afternoon, the Ottawa Rough Riders had defeated the Calgary Stampeders in Toronto. Super Kraut and I had watched the game on TV amidst a room full of Calgary fans. The westerners, including us, were crying in our beer. And there was a lot of beer.

As usual, there was never a dull moment with Super Kraut. He was a blond-haired, blue-eyed, swaggering, hot-shot fighter pilot with movie-star looks and German heritage. Whenever he walked into a room, female conversation screeched to a halt as the women's eyes followed him. For the last two weeks, I had been his "wingman," basking in his reflected glow. I was not a pilot, but a lowly engineer, and thus could never achieve the esteemed status accorded him, even if I had the looks, which I didn't. Together, we had been on an assignment from our home base in Comox, B.C., investigating the crash of one of the air force's—and the world's—fastest aircraft, a CF104 Starfighter jet, aptly called the "widowmaker." We had wrapped up the investigation and were now enjoying our last day at the prairie base.

Super Kraut's female admirers flocked to our dinner table following the football game. Fuelled by the beer, everyone was in a party mood.

"So, this is your last night," Nurse Brenda said, her head down. She was a little dejected, since she had glued herself to Super Kraut over the last several days. She was a nurse in the base hospital, single, and exceptionally gorgeous, with green eyes, auburn hair, and pouting lips. We called her Red for short. "We should liven things up."

"Yeah, great idea," Nurse Judy said. She was Red's sidekick, the nurse version of a wingman. She and I had become friends, not intimate ones, more drinking buddies. She was no slouch in the looks department either: curvy, blonde, and buxom, hence her nickname Jugs. She smiled a lot. I was happy to have reaped the rewards found in Super Kraut's glow. "Let's play crud," she said.

Like Ben, I said, "What's crud?"

"You guys are from a fighter base and you've never heard of crud?" she said, with a slight sneer.

"No, but then we don't have ten months of winter to waste inside, either," Super Kraut said, showing his pearly whites in a Cheshire cat smile.

Red snickered but countered. "Hey, those are ten good months. We invented the game in Cold Lake because of them. All the Americans and Brits love it when they come here."

"How do you play it?" I said.

"Well, first you need a snooker table," said Red, "and then …"

"Two balls—the cue ball and one striped ball." Jugs finished her sentence.

"Pretty simple," I said. "Even fighter pilots can count that high." I winked at Super Kraut, who looked down his nose at me.

"Whadda ya do with them?" he said.

"You divide into teams and each person takes a turn trying to hit the striped ball into a pocket with the cue ball," Red said.

"Yeah, but you gotta do it only from the ends of the table and only by throwing it. No pool cues allowed," Jugs said.

"If the striped ball stops moving before you hit it you lose a life," Red said.

"And if the person after you knocks the striped ball into a pocket, you lose a life," Jugs said. "You have three lives. When they're gone, it's bye-bye."

"Losers buy the beer," said Red. "Part of the rules."

Super Kraut leaned back in his chair, stretched out his legs, and put his arms behind his head. "Should be a snap," he said. "C'mon, Doogie. Let's take 'em on. Cold Lake against Comox. We'll have free beer for the rest of the night."

I was suckered in. Anything with these girls was worth it. "Sure, why not, we'll smoke 'em," I said, as I watched the girls exchange knowing smiles.

"You're on," Red said. "Let's grab the table."

We all got up, beer glasses in hand. Super Kraut and I walked arm-in-arm with the girls down the stairs to the bar and pool room.

The bar was full of smoke. Everyone was standing. Like us, the guys all wore flight suits. Baritone-voiced pilots danced make-believe dogfights with their arms. Super Kraut recognized two of them, Howler and Chicken Little from Comox. They were here to fly us both home tomorrow in T-33 trainer jets. They were explaining to Kate, one of the local single schoolteachers, the manoeuvre they would use to shoot down a Russian Bear bomber from their Voodoo interceptors. She stifled a yawn, then spotted us.

"Hey, guys, what's goin' on?"

"We're gonna teach these crud rookies how to play. Wanna join us?" Jugs asked. "You can be on our team."

"Sure."

"OK, we get Howler, then," Super Kraut said. "Hey, Chicken Little, you can be the ref." Chicken Little was short and slight, more like a jockey than a pilot. His stature didn't affect his prowess as a pilot, though. He was reputed to be fearless, always one of the best at the annual Top Gun air combat competition, where the movie got its name.

"Done," Chicken Little said. "My first ruling is that it's a full contact game." He'd played before.

"Whoa, cowboy, what's full contact?" I said. The girls hadn't mentioned this.

"Nothin' serious," Red said. "Just that you can use your body to block anyone trying to reach the cue ball. You're not gonna get cold feet, now, are you Doogie?" Her green eyes smiled at me.

Crashing occasionally into the softness of three curvaceous femmes fatales in form-fitting slacks and sweaters may not be so bad, I thought. "Nah, course not," I said.

Our expanded group moved into the pool room. There were three big snooker tables; two were occupied and the third, only used for crud, sat forlornly in a dark corner, its green felt cushions tattered. Ugly beer stains covered half the surface. We turned the lights on over it. That's when

Jugs laid her head on the surface, stretched out her arms, and cooed, "Hi, baby. Mama's here. Did you miss me?"

That worried me.

Meanwhile, Chicken Little wrote the team names on the blackboard beside the table. Our team's lineup was Howler, me, and Super Kraut. The girls were Schoolie, Kate, Jugs, and Red.

We refilled our drinks, then got ready as Chicken Little reviewed the finer points of the game.

"OK, listen up," he said. "No walking on the table; ya gotta keep one foot on the floor at all times. You can't dispute the ref's ruling. Oh, yeah, if a player spills the ref's drink, he hasta buy him another one. That's it. You know the rest. Let's go."

Schoolie opened as the rest of us stood at the sides of the table. Howler received, which meant he waited at the far end of the table for Schoolie's cue ball to hit the striped ten ball. It did. With deadly accuracy. The ten slowly rolled toward the left corner pocket as the cue ball skittered back to Schoolie's end of the table.

"Oh, shit," Howler said as he ran along my side of the table chasing the cue ball. Reaching Schoolie's end, he grabbed the ball and threw it backhand down to the other end. It hit the cushion just as the ten disappeared into the corner pocket.

"Howler loses a life," Chicken Little said.

"Sonuva B!" Howler cursed and hit the table with his hand.

The girls all high-fived each other. "Way to go, Schoolie!" Jugs said, beaming.

"Lucky shot," said Super Kraut, laughing it off. "We're still gonna wipe you girls off the map."

Next up was Jugs, who served to me. She hit the ten just off centre and both balls rolled back to her end. I chased the cue ball and caught up with it midway down the table. At the end I let go of it with a light push. It nudged the ten about three inches before it stopped.

Red, next in the lineup, didn't even try to retrieve the cue ball. "No six," she said, holding her thumb and pinkie on the track travelled by the ten.

"What?" I screamed. "What the hell is a six? That was a clean shot."

"Clean, yeah, but the ten didn't go far enough. It's gotta travel at least six inches," Red said. "You know, the average size of a guy's pe…"

Chicken Little interrupted, "I hate to say this, but Doogie loses a life."

Red smirked at me. "Read the rules," she said, waving her finger at a faded typewritten paper on the wall by the blackboard. "Not knowing them's no excuse."

She then served to Super Kraut. He stood upright at the end of the table, his arms folded across his chest. He was cocky. "There's no way you're gonna hit this ball, darlin'," he said. "It's too far away."

Crack! The two balls connected and rolled back up the table. Super Kraut unfolded his arms and stared at them. I could see his mind calculating where they were going to end up. He started to run down Chicken Little's side of the table, staring at the two balls. Unfortunately, he forgot

Chicken Little was there. They collided. Both remained standing but Chicken Little's drink headed for the floor.

"OK, that's a life *and* a drink," Chicken Little said. "Time out while you buy me one."

"Hey, I thought you were on *our* side," Super Kraut said.

"Yeah, but a drink's more important than loyalty."

All the guys had now lost lives. Not a good start.

"So, how do you *Comox* boys like crud so far?" Jugs asked. "Not so easy, is it?" She wiggled her butt, taunting us.

"Steep learning curve but we'll get it," I said, "and then watch out."

Within the next twenty minutes, we *sort* of got it. We managed to knock a life off each of our opponents, more through dumb luck than skill.

Schoolie lost a life when she ran across the table to retrieve the cue ball. She'd just downed her sixth beer and forgot the rules.

Jugs lost a life when she missed her turn, distracted by a handsome helicopter pilot who had joined the party as a spectator.

Red lost a life legitimately when Super Kraut actually put the ten in a side pocket before Schoolie could reach the cue ball and save her.

In the same time, *we* all lost another life. We were going down fast. We had to do something. From here on it was serious—and it got physical.

I stood in the way of Schoolie as she tore up one side of the table trying to catch the cue ball before the ten dribbled into a side pocket courtesy of an ace shot by Howler. She danced around me but didn't make it in time.

But then things backfired.

The next serve was hers and I retrieved. Schoolie nicked the ten with the cue ball, and as I started my charge up the side of the table to catch the cue ball, I noticed stomach flesh and the tantalizing hint of bare breasts on the far side. They belonged to Red. I turned my head in disbelief and hit the smoothly rounded butt directly in front of me at full tilt, crumpling to the floor with a groan.

I shook my head and rubbed a bruised thigh. Shit, I'd never been hit harder than that even in hockey. So much for soft curves.

Jugs grinned down at me. "Nice try, Doogie. It's called teamwork. You know, T-E-A-M."

I pulled myself upright and shouted at Chicken Little. "Hey, ref, that was illegal flashing. Red should lose a life."

My teammates agreed. They raised their glasses and chanted in unison, "Life, life, life, life, life."

Chicken Little succumbed. "OK, ref's prerogative. Red loses a life." Lucky for us he wasn't totally impartial. The girls harassed him for five minutes, but he stood his ground, determined to make this a fair fight.

In the next round we managed to knock Schoolie out of the game, but she was too drunk to continue anyway. Howler went down. Then it was just the four of us from dinner.

After that, Jugs served to me and I got lucky. I grabbed the cue ball right off her serve and just tipped the ten so it moved snail-like across the felt. The cue ball bounced erratically off the cushion toward the far end. Red realized she had a great distance to cover to reach it before the ten stopped moving.

Meanwhile, Super Kraut had taken up a position at the end of the table where the ten was. He hovered over it, arms waving in an effort to distract Red. "Lady, you don't have a chance. You're goin' down, down, down." As he said this, he slowly crouched down on his haunches until he was at eye level with the ten.

Red flew low around the far corner, grabbed the cue ball, and let it go side-arm. It took one bounce over the ten and with a resounding thwack hit Super Kraut dead centre in the forehead.

It was quite amazing how much attention two nurses— and a drunken school teacher—could pay to one patient.

Super Kraut was flat on his back. Schoolie stumbled to the bar for an ice pack while Jugs and Red cradled his head in their arms. We all watched as his goose egg grew larger.

"Ohh, that's gotta smart," Howler said. "He's gonna feel it when he wakes up."

Chicken Little took the opportunity to make his final pronouncement. "Illegal throw. Man down. Comox wins."

The girls didn't care. They had other things to do.

When Super Kraut finally regained consciousness about five minutes later, his eyes were crossed. It was the first time I'd seen him dishevelled, not to mention disoriented. "Ow, my frickin' head." He felt the bump. "Wha happened?" he said.

"You had a nasty fall," Red said. It was her calming nurse voice. "We're going to take you to the hospital for an x-ray."

Howler and I started to blurt out the truth, then looked at each other. We didn't want to jeopardize the free beer owed us as the winners.

Jugs and Red left for the base hospital, supporting Super Kraut between them. Schoolie toddled at their heels, hoping at some point to have a reason to touch the golden boy.

Howler, Chicken Little, and I stayed behind. By 11:30, we decided to call it a night as the girls hadn't returned. We never did get our free beer.

* * *

Ben stared at me for a long time. "Do you know what the word 'liability' means?" he finally asked.

"Yeah, of course," I said. "Somebody has to accept responsibility for injuries or theft and what not."

"Any idea who that might be if we let our clients play crud?"

"Uh, well, uh, maybe … no, I don't."

"Well, I can tell you," he said. "For sure there's no damn way it's going to be our insurance company."

"I guess that means you don't like the idea?"

"You got *that* right, sport."

Chapter Six

Talent

The job of our entertainment agency was simple: buy and sell talent. These entities with talent—not always human—inhabited strange worlds that sometimes collided with our rather tedious one. Then the job got really interesting.

* * *

Table acts were some of the mainstays of our roster. They were people who literally sat at tables and performed for our guests, usually one-on-one at receptions. They included caricaturists, card sharps, handwriting analysts, palm readers, tarot card readers, sleight-of-hand magicians, silhouette artists, and a whole menu of others that really knew how to keep a party moving.

One of these was a lady named Princess White Buffalo. She was a Mandan Indian from the northern United States, in her late fifties and a little overweight, but very friendly and outgoing. I first met her at an important corporate party Ben had arranged. I was helping with the acts and getting them in place before the event started. This night she was dressed in a long, cream-coloured leather dress adorned with coloured bead highlights. She also had a beautiful turquoise necklace. Her specialty was Indian fortune sticks.

"Would you like your fortune read?" she asked me, since we had some time to kill.

"Sure, why not." I had never really believed in this stuff even though I promoted it like crazy to our clients.

She rolled the long, painted, wooden sticks around in her hands, then dropped them randomly on the table. They ended up all over, looking a lot like a slightly enlarged version of the kids' game Pick-Up-Sticks.

She paused for a minute, thinking quietly.

"You have a good life and a nice family with children," she said.

OK, I thought, no particular revelation there.

"But I'm reading something else, something unusual," she said. "You and I have some kind of past connection. I don't know what it is but it's definitely there."

"I have no idea," I said. "Other than booking you as an act, I'm pretty sure we haven't met."

I left with the unanswered question in the back of my mind. A few days later, while combing through the promotional files of our acts, I came across hers. In it was a black and white photo of a gorgeous young Indian maiden dressed head-to-toe in white buckskin with a full feather headdress. She was sitting atop a rearing white stallion. It was a classic pose for an act that might have come right out of Buffalo Bill's Wild West Show.

"Is this Princess White Buffalo?" I asked Ben.

"Sure is."

"She doesn't look like that anymore."

"No, it's an old photo from a few years ago. Great promo, isn't it?

"Yeah, but why the horse and everything?"

"She used to have a knife-and-whip act with her husband, so she had to dress the part. The horse added to the spectacle."

I imagined the beautiful princess tied to a tree with knives flying around her head. The whips, though, were harder to picture. Maybe putting out cigarettes in her mouth or something equally dangerous.

"She and her husband split up ten or twelve years ago," Ben said.

I wondered if the whips might have missed their mark a few too many times.

"She lives with her daughter and granddaughter now," he continued, "and she only does the fortune stick thing, no more whips and knives."

"This is weird," I said, "but I think I've seen her before—and not just at the gig a few days ago."

The memory came from somewhere in the distant past. I went home that evening and searched through some old photo albums. Sure enough, I found a picture. Princess White Buffalo was smiling at the camera. She was stunning. My father had taken the picture of her at a powwow in North Vancouver back when I was about nine or ten, some thirty years previously. I had befriended a young Indian boy and we were running around amongst the teepees when we saw her. She stood out from the crowd in her white buckskins and feathers. I told my father and he rushed to get a shot of her. Only trouble was, she was on crutches. It seemed odd and we never did find out why.

About a week later, we booked her again. I showed her the old photo my father had taken.

"My dad was absolutely smitten with you," I said. "Why were you on crutches?"

She was almost speechless. "What a coincidence! You know that promo picture of me on the horse?"

"Yeah, it's an amazing shot."

"Well, right after he reared up, I fell off and broke my leg. We had to continue our tour of powwows and fairs, so I still dressed up in my regalia and hobbled around with my crutches."

"I guess you were right," I said.

She just smiled

The circle was complete. It was in the sticks all along.

* * *

Celebrity worship has been around since the time of the ancient Egyptians and Greeks, but the latter-day popularity of celebrity lookalikes and impersonators always baffled me. People went crazy over them, almost as much as the real thing, and nobody was crazier than Elvis impersonator fans.

We had four or five singing "Elvii" on our roster, including a nine-year-old Philippino boy. Audiences loved him because he was just plain cute. They clapped politely for him, as was befitting a star of that age. Their reaction wasn't quite the same for the adult impersonators. No, for them every middle-aged grandmother and pistol-packin' country mama for miles around somehow sensed there was an Elvis in the vicinity. They screamed. They swarmed the stage. They cried just to touch the performer. Lucky ones caught a scarf tossed frivolously into the crowd. I used to wonder what kind of warped childhood they had had.

But the childhood of the fans was not as strange as the childhood of the impersonators. I don't know how, but most of them said they had been given a message that they were destined to impersonate the king. Maybe their parents gave them the message. Maybe those parents dressed them up as the child version of their saviour—like the Philippino kid. Maybe they just received the message through the ether.

One of ours, a fellow in his mid-twenties, was mediocre as an impersonator at best, but he admittedly grew up glued to his parents' record player listening to Elvis tunes. By the time he was in his teens he knew them all. His parents must have convinced him he had that certain destiny.

Unfortunately, he wanted to make sure that we knew it. He made frequent visits to our office to remind us. I never saw him attired in anything but a white jumpsuit. It was hard to imagine he would spend his days dressed like this, but who knows. I guess it was his way of evangelizing. As I said, this was a different breed.

Sandy, a new receptionist I had hired, learned about him the hard way. She had been with us for about two weeks when Elvis appeared late on a Friday afternoon. His white ensemble was augmented with dark shades and a long red scarf, his dyed black hair swept up and back in Brylcreem perfection. He usually entered the office and immediately burst out with, "Hey, man, the king is here." Today he entered but did a little double take as he spotted Sandy behind the reception desk. His brain made a few hasty new connections. There was another human as attractive as he was. He tried a different opening line.

"Whoa, pretty lady. The king is heah to whisk you off yaw feet." It was his best attempt at a southern baritone drawl.

He broke into a cappella song. "Love me tender, love me sweet ..."

Sandy smiled.

"Never let me go ..."

Elvis leaned on the reception desk and peered over at her. He smoothed his hair back with a deft wrist flick.

Sandy's eyes started to sparkle.

"You have made ma luff complete, and ah love you so."

Elvis slithered around the end of the reception desk and got down on one knee beside Sandy's chair.

Her face turned red.

"Love me tender, love me true, all ma dreams fulfill; for ma darlin' ah love you, and ah alwaaaaays will." He finished with a flourish, arms in the air. Then he ripped off his scarf and gave it to Sandy.

She clapped politely. "Ohh, that's so sweet! Thank you."

As Elvis got up she looked over at me and rolled her eyes. That was my cue.

"Well, I see you two are getting along. I have a meeting in fifteen minutes so I have to get out of here. Remember to lock up. And play nicely. See you Monday, Sandy."

"Hey, man, don't forget, Elvis is always available."

Quite the salesman, I thought.

I arrived early on Monday. Sandy came in half an hour later and stormed into my office. She was furious.

"You left me all alone with that creep."

"What happened? I thought you were getting along OK."

"Are you kidding? He wouldn't stop. He must have sung a dozen songs—and they were all pretty bad. I couldn't shut him up."

"Geez, I'm sorry, Sandy. He usually doesn't stay long. He must have taken a liking to you. Did he make any moves, touching or anything?"

"Naw, but every time I got up to go, he said, 'Just one more song, pretty lady.' I don't ever want to see him again. I got home two hours late."

"OK, I'll take care of it." I called Elvis and told him he really didn't need to come by the office so much. Just call me occasionally.

Sandy was happy with that. I purposely didn't tell her about Tina, Rod, Cher, Neil, and the others.

* * *

For one national convention, we had to design an after-dinner show about communications that transitioned from the past into the present. We had an actor who was costumed as Lord Strathcona, the man who drove the last spike to complete the transcontinental Canadian Pacific Railway in 1885, and we had to somehow segue from him into a stage show with three female vocalists from modern times.

John, one of our producers, said, "Let's use pyro." He doubled as a masterful magician and frequently added to his shows with explosions onstage. I figured he knew his stuff.

"What do you propose?" I asked.

"Line rockets and flashpots."

By this time I'd been in show biz for ten years. I knew about these things. Line rockets were fireworks on pre-strung, almost invisible wires. They whistled and flew across a room, often no more than two or three feet above the audience's heads. They invariably scared the living stuffing out of people. Flashpots were small metal cups filled with gunpowder. Their purpose was to make a huge explosion and generate a lot of smoke. If the rockets didn't traumatize, the flashpots did. I thought for a moment. Raising the adrenalin level of the audience may just work. It sounded exciting.

"OK," I said, "how would you set them up?"

"Here's my plan. First, we have Lord Strathcona hit our spike with his mallet and that'll set off a line rocket from the base of the spike up to the satellite in the ceiling. Then three more line rockets zip down wires from there to the top of three magic doors onstage."

We had built a six-foot-tall replica golden spike and a ten-foot-tall foam mallet just for the occasion, plus a fake satellite. It was all supposed to be a symbolic transition in time. This would be impressive, I thought.

"That's cool. Safe for the audience. How do the doors work?" I'd seen them used before but was clueless about how they functioned.

"Well, you put the doors against a black stage backdrop because they have black roll-up curtains on springs, so it looks like they're really just open doorframes against the stage backdrop. You put one flashpot in front of each door. I stand beside the stage out of view and when the rockets reach the top of the doors, I use a cable release to pop the door curtains and a switch to set off the flashpots."

"So from that I assume we have to put the girls *behind* the doors before anything happens?" The girls were the three vocalists who would supposedly magically appear.

"Right, but they won't be seen because we can keep the main stage curtain closed until Lord Strathcona's ready to start." John had it all figured out. I had to give him credit. It was a brilliant idea.

I took it to my client. "What do you think?" I asked.

"It sounds good, but just make sure the girls are dressed conservatively." She was a matronly fuss-budget. She continually fretted about her group, mostly middle-aged male executives and their spouses. There was no hint of concern about the pyro.

"Great. Thanks," I said. "We'll get to work."

Lord Strathcona looked perfect. He sported a shiny top hat, long white beard, and full morning suit, a fitting ensemble for an 1880s railway executive. As he raised the giant mallet over his head, I thought for a second that he might topple over, but he recovered and brought it down squarely on the giant golden spike.

"Bang! Wheeeeeeeee …!" The line rocket screeched to the satellite in the ceiling.

The audience gasped.

"Wheeeee … Wheeee … Wheeeee …" Three more line rockets sped down toward the doors onstage.

"KABOOOOM!" A giant flame shot up from in front of each magic door and the entire stage was engulfed in a cloud of smoke.

The audience jumped in their seats. I heard one or two screams. Luckily, nobody fainted.

We waited. Where are the girls? I thought, as the backing tracks to their song "Fire" started.

Four or five seconds later I heard the faint sound of female voices struggling to sing in harmony.

Then they appeared, staggering through the dissipating smoke. The three of them were wearing *very* short, slinky silver dresses. In fact, they could have been negligees. It looked like a bomb had landed in the middle of a brothel. Maybe I should have made the dress thing a little clearer, I thought.

They regained their composure and finished the show to generous applause.

After, I went backstage.

John was apologetic. "Geez, I put way too much powder in the flashpots. Sorry about that."

"Yeah, it was so loud we could barely hear the music. I think we lost our hearing for a couple of seconds," Kathy shouted. She was the leader of the singers. "*And* you forgot to tell us about the rockets. We thought we were going to die when we saw them coming toward us."

"Sorry," I said. I gave John a reproving look.

"Shit! I *knew* I forgot something." He looked remorseful. This was obviously part of our learning curve about pyro.

"You're forgiven. But only 'cause it was funny, too," she said. "It'll be a story for us to tell." The girls all laughed.

That wasn't the end of my problems, though.

When I went back out front, my client was waiting. She scowled at me.

"I thought I told you to make sure the girls were dressed appropriately," she said. "They looked like hookers."

I repressed a smile, reminded of the bombed brothel image. I tried to look contrite. "I apologize. I should have been more emphatic with them."

Just as I said this, a couple of male audience members walked by.

"Great show, Doug."

"Loved the girls. They were fantastic."

My client walked away.

I didn't know whether to laugh or cry.

* * *

And God said, "Let the earth bring forth every kind of animal" … Then God said, "Let us make people … They will be masters over … wild animals." (Gen. 1:24–26) Unfortunately, humans put the animals in places they should never have been.

I had a friend whose talent we often bought. His name was Gary and he supplied animals of every description for the movies. Out of the blue one day, he came to our office.

"Doug, Doug, I've got some big cats in town for a movie." He could barely contain his excitement. "They're only here for three weeks. If you want, I could bring them to one of your events. Do you have anything on the go?"

I thought for a moment. "Yeah, I might have. A big convention in Whistler in two weeks. Tell me about the cats."

Gary had a bushy, handlebar moustache that bounced when he talked and blue eyes that twinkled when he was excited. Everything was bouncing and twinkling today. "Oh, you won't believe this," he said. He showed me some fuzzy Polaroid photos. "Aren't they beautiful? The little tiger cub's only two months old. The panther's a juvenile, still not full grown. I have handlers who can stay with them. Your clients will love them. They can even pet them. Think of it. It'll blow them away."

His timing couldn't have been better. We were in the middle of putting the finishing touches on the entertainment for a convention with the theme "Around the World in Eighty Hours," a takeoff on the Jules Verne classic, "Around the World in Eighty Days." The last night was to be a wildly creative offering of entertainment from the various countries Phileas Fogg and Passepartout visited on their trip. The animals would be perfect for India.

"Let's do it," I said. "The handlers will have to dress up as Hindus and stay at their post for about four hours. It's a reception and buffet, so the guests will be circulating." I knew my client would like the once-in-a-lifetime opportunity.

It was ten minutes to doors opening for the Around the World extravaganza. I waited with the handlers and cats, who sat docilely on the floor. The handlers were stroking them. Gary was right. They really were beautiful. The baby tiger was perhaps three feet long. He had enormous paws. The panther was about four or five feet long with silky black fur and gleaming eyes. The night was going to be an unforgettable experience.

The tiger's handler was a young guy. He looked fairly strong. The panther's handler was a petite blonde. I had to ask her the question.

"Are you sure you can manage him?"

"Oh, yeah, no problem," she said. "He knows me. We're buddies."

Stop worrying, I thought. Everything will be fine.

We sat in silence for a few more minutes, admiring the animals and watching the wait staff bring their final loads of fresh food to buffet tables around the room. Then it happened.

A waiter with a tall cart full of dishes bumped the cart over a power cable taped across the floor. The rattling dishes broke the stillness.

I used to watch Tarzan movies as a kid and often wondered what it would be like to be jumped by a jungle cat in the wild. At that moment, I was given a pretty good idea. You wouldn't stand a chance.

The panther could have been a rocket. I'd never seen any living thing move so fast. In less than a breath he was on top of the cart and accelerating toward a table. He pounced. The table crashed to the floor, breaking dishes and spreading linens and cutlery all over.

His handler said in a high-pitched, childlike voice, "Oh my god! He's never done that before." She started to sprint across the room, losing ground to the cat's Mach two slink.

The panther reached the stage at the far end of the room and slowed down. She caught up, grabbed his leash, and dragged him back, speaking softly to him, "Bad kitty. You be good from now on."

I wasn't entirely convinced that would be enough to keep him calm for the whole night.

Luckily, nothing else was damaged, but by now, everybody was in panic mode. The wait staff were running all over, gathering up broken dishes and resetting the smashed table. The catering manager shouted at me, "This could be a disaster." His eyes were wide. He looked terrified. "You can't keep the animals here."

I took a deep breath. "Listen," I said, "the client's been looking forward to this. Let me just tell him there's a slight delay and the doors will open in five minutes."

"I don't know," he said. "It could still be dangerous."

"The handlers tell me what happened was really unusual. They're convinced the cats will be fine," I lied.

He reluctantly agreed, and five minutes later the doors opened.

The cats were the hit of the party. Everybody got to pet them. Thousands of photos were taken. My client was ecstatic. He never knew what happened.

I sweated bullets for four hours.

* * *

Vancouver has always had vibrant ethnic communities. We frequently took advantage of this by hiring some of the dozens of acts that represented world cultures. For one large stand-up reception, we created a show of Asia-Pacific acts. There was quite a variety: dancers, musicians, magic. Before the show, I talked to the "mother hen" of a duo of Japanese koto lute players—her protégés—who were to provide background music throughout the event. Her name was Theresa.

"The girls will be fine," she said. "Just tell them when to start and stop playing and they'll do what you say."

The "girls" were two pretty Japanese musicians, fully attired in colourful kimonos. They couldn't have been more than fourteen and were possessed of innocent smiles. They played their stringed instruments from a kneeling position on the floor at the back of the stage. Once they tuned up, I realized they were excellent musicians as well.

"Don't worry, Theresa, I'll take good care of them," I said. I knew the whole event was pretty straightforward. All I had to do was get the acts on and off the stage at the appointed times. Nothing complicated.

A Chinese lion came and went, accompanied by clanging cymbals and a pounding drum. Hawaiian dancers strutted their stuff and even brought some audience members onstage to try the hula. The koto lutes played mostly in between the main acts. At about 8:45 p.m., it was time to bring out the final act.

"Stay onstage and play through this last act," I said to the koto players. "There's not much talking and I think it'll make for a nice background."

I had chosen this final act carefully because it was visually appealing. "The Amazing Jozef." I knew it would be the highlight of the evening. However, Jozef himself wasn't the appeal. He was an elderly magician, well past his prime. No, part of the appeal was his voluptuous assistant whom I'll call Jeannie because she was the spitting image of Jeannie in the old TV show, "I Dream of Jeannie." Her diaphanous outfit helped with the comparison—and the appeal.

The other part of the appeal was Peter, a twenty-foot python.

As I squeezed through the crowd to bring Jozef and his entourage up to the stage, I asked about Peter.

"Is he going to be OK?" Peter was wrapped around Jeannie, looking a little frightened. At least he did to me, but what did I know about a snake's emotions.

"He's just getting warmed up to the crowd," said Jeannie. She stroked his greenish white body. Peter stared at me and flicked his tongue several times. I still thought he looked scared. Or maybe he was hungry.

"Has he been fed?" I asked.

"He gets stage fright," she said. "He doesn't like to eat before a performance."

Aha, I *was* right. "You've gotta be kidding." I remembered that pythons fed on birds and small mammals, killing them by squeezing them to death. They didn't usually attack humans unless startled or provoked. I knew sudden movement would do that.

"Don't worry." Jeannie read my frown. "He's done the act dozens of times. Peter's a stage vet. Aren't you, pookie?" She stroked his head as he started to slither into a new position around her neck. "We'll feed him some yummies after the show."

We made it to the stage, where the kotos were continuing as musical wallpaper.

However, the combination of beauty—Jeannie—and potential terror—Peter—immediately brought a huge crowd to the edge of the stage. I was instantly trapped. Nowhere to go. I felt rather helpless as Jozef, dressed in a vague tribute to things Arab, slowly mounted the stairs followed by Jeannie and Peter. I knew that what happened next was out of my control.

Jozef performed a number of old but uniquely conceived illusions, and alternately worked with Jeannie and the python, gradually building toward the show's climax, as the kotos kept playing behind them. It looked good. The crowd was, as expected, mesmerized. For his final illusion, Jozef made a brief announcement.

"Ladies and gentlemen, for my final illusion, from the sands of ancient Arabia, here is *The Sword of Ali Baba!*"

So *that's* why he's dressed like that, I thought.

Jozef purposely milked the crowd's attention, playing a little longer than he should have. It seemed like forever, until he managed to place a horizontally rigid Jeannie atop a vertical, unsupported scimitar.

Unfortunately, Peter wasn't part of the finale.

My attention was focused on Jeannie, who was up in the air and not easy to miss. Peter was on the floor, out of the limelight. He was easier to miss. Certainly the audience had forgotten about him. Out of sight, out of mind, I guess.

I glanced down. Yup, there was Peter. But he wasn't stationary. He'd decided to explore. Upstage. Toward the back. Where the girls were. Maybe he was just inquisitive. I had a sudden sinking feeling. He was probably hungry, in fact starved by now. After all, he'd finished his part, and he was expecting "yummies."

I watched dumbstruck as the gap between Peter and the koto players narrowed.

My mind raced. If I shouted at the girls and told them to run off stage, Peter might get startled and get his yummies early. If I shouted at Jozef, he might lose his concentration and Jeannie would fall, probably injuring herself and ruining the show. If I tried to get onstage and grab Peter … well, that was definitely out of the question. I chose to just stay put and pray.

It was a good thing that nobody was well acquainted with koto music. The girls kept playing, but they were no longer reading their music. They were just staring at Peter. And Peter was staring back, flicking his tongue and moving his head from side to side as if trying to keep time to their music. He slithered closer. Their eyes by now resembled anime characters, huge and, in this case, terrified. They were on the verge of tears.

Peter was now about half a metre away from them.

Suddenly I saw a hand reach down and scoop Peter up. It was Jozef. Jozef the saviour. Jozef the most amazing, most mesmerizing, most awesome magician in the world. Thank you, Jozef, I whispered to myself.

After the show, Jeannie let everybody stroke Peter. "Isn't he wonderful?" she said. "See, he's not slimy at all, not what you might imagine." He seemed to enjoy it, utterly oblivious to the trauma he had caused two young musicians.

I did wonder later, though, why Theresa never returned any of my calls for future gigs.

Chapter Seven

Dreams of Gold

I liked Alan from the moment we met. In his late twenties, he was one of those gentle giant types—tall, muscular, canyon-voiced, and gregarious. His rugged face could turn elastically in an instant from a look of utter sadness to unabashed joy. He was the kind of person anyone would have wanted for a big brother. I first came to know him as a playwright. He had just completed a whimsical musical about a couple who met on their journey up the Cariboo Wagon Road in the 1870s. They had dreams of striking it rich in the gold fields of British Columbia. Alan was in our office for a meeting of the cast. Ben introduced us.

"So you're Alan," I said. "Your play's great. It's got everything; love, humour, drama—and I really like the music." Not only was the play original, but most of the music was too, written in the style of the era. I truly was impressed. But Alan was humble.

"Yeah, thanks. I'm just a simple actor who loves to write," he said in a slow rumble, "but Ben thinks it still needs a lot of work."

"Well, the old boy can be grumpy and twisted but he has your best interest at heart." I glanced at Ben behind his giant mahogany desk. He frowned. "Listen to his advice, though, and it'll be even better than it is now. I think our audiences are going to love it. It really tugs at the heart-strings. Everyone can relate to pursuing their dreams."

"Well, I sure hope so. It would be good to have a successful play. Hey, I hear you're going to be our boss for the summer."

"I am. I think it's going to be a trial by fire, though. I've never been a theatre manager before."

Our company had the contract to produce two original plays each summer at the Theatre Royal in Barkerville, the old town that used to be the centre of the gold rush. The town was now restored and a major tourist attraction. Ben had decided that my training in "show biz" could use some hands-on experience as the manager of the theatre. I was to take my wife and kids there to live for the summer.

"Don't worry," Alan said. "We'll go easy on you. Besides, Barkerville's an adventure. There's lots to do—fishing, canoeing, hiking. It's perfect for your family." He'd been there before as an actor and loved the outdoors.

"Thanks. I'll let them know. We'll see you there in a few weeks." What a positive guy, I thought. He's going to make my job a lot easier.

Barkerville once was reputed to be the "biggest town north of San Francisco and west of Chicago." That was in the 1870s in the middle of the Cariboo Gold Rush, when it was full of an eclectic potpourri of dreamers from the United States and the British Isles, plus a handful of Canadians and Chinese. One hundred and fifteen years later, the total annual population—mostly summer tourists now—was about the same as it had been then. But nobody stayed longer than a couple of months, those being concession staff and actors in period costumes. It was easy to understand why. Even though the town was part of the reason behind the province of B.C. joining the Canadian confederation, its popularity as a "home" rapidly deteriorated with the dwindling gold. But this was not just because of the gold. It was simply not a nice place to live.

We found that out quickly. Arriving by car in mid-June through a "twilight zone"-type of thunderstorm that carried us back over a hundred years in time, we landed at what was basically still the edge of the wilderness, almost four thousand feet up in the western foothills of the Rocky Mountains. Tall pines and cedars draped the steep hill that hugged the west side of town. The town itself ran in two parallel streets lined with mostly single-storey wooden buildings, some restored and painted, some still proudly sporting the silvered seniority of aged cedar. A wide, grassy bench ran along the other side of town, and this dropped steeply into William's Creek where gold was discovered by the stumpy Englishman, Billy Barker, in 1862. It still gurgled its promises of boundless wealth. Save for the town's concessions and the campground just outside, there were few modern amenities. To top things off, the short summer had three sub-seasons: cold rain and no-see-ums (June); moderately warm showers and mosquitoes (July); and warm sun and horse flies (August). The only other seasons of the year that we had heard about—but fortunately didn't have to live through—were heavy rain (usually cold) and snow (frigid). There was nothing otherwise definable in terms of the seasons we knew on the coast in Vancouver.

My wife was not impressed. After our first night, she said, "Look at this," pointing to several finger-sized holes in the window screens of the dusty trailer that was our home for the summer. "No wonder we all have dozens of bites. It's the no-see-ums." Everyone had numerous red welts around their necks and ankles. The itching was relentless, the crazed scratching a physical activity that resembled intense arm aerobics.

"Let's try covering the holes over with duct tape," I suggested, which we did. It didn't work. The next morning there were more bites.

"I'll try some old panty hose," she said. That worked as long as every square inch of screen was covered. We now had a light brownish haze to pass for daylight inside.

"Oh, well, if we can't see outside we can always watch TV," she said. We had brought a small black and white portable with us. I turned it on. We all watched in dismay as it hissed and popped on every channel.

"How about the radio?" she asked, turning on the only other electronic device we had. Cell phones and portable computers were still ten years away. More hissing and static. Finally, the voice of the CBC crackled through the night.

"Ah, a breakthrough!" I shouted.

"Yay, I can listen to the news," my wife said. She hated being out of touch. And indeed, apart from the occasional newspaper bought on our weekly shopping forays to Quesnel, an hour's drive to the west, that was our only source of information about the outside world.

Meanwhile, I had two plays to transform into stage-ready, audience-engrossing theatrical marvels. In ten days. Things were not going particularly well.

As with any summer stock, relationships were developing amongst cast members and problems were surfacing. To complicate things, the distance from civilization was asserting its influence.

Our lighting designer alternated between fits of brilliance and outright angry obstinence. A drunk, he was days behind schedule. To get him to do anything I had to cajole and plead through his girlfriend, our costume designer, thus occasionally pitting them both against me.

One actress was a hypochondriac, which necessitated a long trip to the nearest hospital in Quesnel.

Our very young alternate pianist had crying fits of homesickness. Where were the malls and movie theatres when you needed them? Why couldn't she bring her boy-friend here?

One actor decided a local girl was better company than his wife back home.

The constant rain and bugs didn't help. They frayed nerves and invited complaints.

But one light shone brightly. Alan.

Three days before opening, the director of his play plunged into an especially gruelling rehearsal. After two hours, he called a break to relieve croaking voices and the confusion of constant cue changes. Alan, in his typical style, had written himself into one scene in a self-deprecating role as the rear half of a camel (camels were, at one time, used on the Cariboo Wagon Road). He threw the tail off and emerged sweating.

"OK, you guys," he snarled with a smirk, "there's only room for one asshole in this show and I'm it, so quit your bellyaching." Everyone broke up. The show opened on schedule to profuse applause and laughter in all the right places. He'd kept the cast from devouring each other.

By the middle of July—sub-season number two—my wife and kids had almost adjusted to their sparse, itchy life on the frontier. Our daughter, only eight, was still a little shy, though. I had given her a job of selling programs to theatre patrons as they waited for the shows to begin. Alan saw that she was having trouble and took her aside after one afternoon's show.

"You need a smile," he said. "Watch."

He mounted a unicycle and proceeded to juggle three balls, all the while alternating goofy looks with his rubber face. She giggled under her cute Victorian bonnet.

"You're silly," she said

"Yes, I am," he agreed, "and remember that when you're selling programs. Think of me and smile and ask people if they want to learn all about a really funny show. Then you say, 'It's all in this program.'"

In no time, her sales ballooned and she began to talk to everybody. It was a transition point in her life.

Alan also had a companion, a big golden Labrador named Kelly, with a red bandana.

Every day about 11:00 o'clock, Alan and Kelly trudged up the muddy main street, headed for the theatre. Past the big oak tree and St. Saviour's Anglican Church near the entrance to town, then up to George's smithy shop and Barnard's Express, where they stopped for a chat with tourists buying theatre tickets. Their final stop before the theatre was the bakery. Here, Kelly would confidently trot in and emerge with Alan's lunch, a sourdough sandwich, held gently in his teeth. On their journey, Alan would often spot a jostle of kids on the boardwalk and set up a mini-show in the middle of the street, juggling and cycling. Kelly would work the crowd. Perched on his hind legs he would paw the air, then walk amongst the onlookers holding out his paw for a shake. Alan invariably made a wad of cash and treated his cast to drinks with his earnings.

Our son was a big Kelly fan.

Dressed like an eleven-year-old runaway from Oliver Twist's London, he plied his trade of selling newspapers to tourists up and down Main Street, encountering Kelly and Alan every day. They became fast friends. With our blessing, Alan invited him on a Saturday fishing trip with Kelly and John, another actor. He couldn't say yes fast enough. The huge trout he landed was the hit of his summer.

Yes, things were finally starting to gel. We were getting into the spirit of the gold rush, the wilderness, and the quaint town of Barkerville. And the two plays were running smoothly.

One night everything changed.

The evening began innocently enough with a barbecue near our trailer for most of the casts of both plays. A billion stars beamed down from the blackness of the high mountain sky. Someone had a guitar. It was finally warm.

Near midnight an RCMP car approached. As the doors opened we could see something was wrong. John got out, bedraggled and wet. Kelly followed, his tail between his legs. He was missing his bandana. John came to the edge of the campfire and delivered the most difficult line of his life.

"Alan's missing."

The Cariboo River begins as a trickle high in glaciers southeast of Barkerville. It soon flattens out and meanders leisurely along the southern stretch of the famous Bowron Lakes Canoe Route, where it empties into Lanezi and Sandy Lakes, surrounded by stunning wilderness vistas of the snow-capped Cariboo Mountains. It then turns in a southward direction. After this, its placid personality changes.

We gradually pieced together the story of what had happened.

Two friends in canoes. One dog. Nothing but blue sky, blue water, blue mountains. A serene summer Saturday. A wilderness for the taking.

Four hours into the trip, the river felt different, stronger. A gentle whisper of white noise was now mixing with bird chitters. A hiss, distant, but growing louder. A thin white line stretched across the horizon between banks of dark green where the rest of the river should have been.

Kelly knew what it was.

He stood up in the canoe and whined. Alan grabbed his bandana, trying to calm him. Kelly pulled to get his friend out. But Alan didn't understand. *He* pulled to keep his friend in. The bandana came loose in Alan's hands. Kelly jumped. His dog legs pumped against the current as he swam for the rocky shore, a mere ten feet away.

John followed from his canoe. They both made it.

John screamed, "Alan, get out!"

Bewildered, Alan turned to them, and then disappeared as the wild hiss enveloped him.

Frantic crashing through undergrowth. John. Kelly. Stumbling down the hill beside the falls. Kelly barking—mournful, plaintive—not a regular bark. John shouting. The roar of the falls gobbled up his voice, as they crashed over shiny, black boulders the size of small cars. At the bottom the churning water revealed nothing. No canoe. No Alan.

Despair.

They continued downriver. It ran swiftly, much faster than they could run through the dense bush. Finally, hours later, they gave up. The early evening sun was streaming in dusty, horizontal beams through the evergreens. Time to head west to the road. Maybe a search team could do better. For John, the mere contemplation of the news he must soon deliver was unbearable.

Actors are emotional beings. *Imagining* reality and its attendant emotions makes them good at their craft. *Experiencing* reality and its emotions confounds them. Tonight, after John's announcement, they were confounded. A sense of disbelief mixed with hope, hope that Alan would be found alive, grounded them for a day. When he wasn't, those emotions ran amok.

I made the dreaded phone call to Ben in Vancouver.

"I have some bad news," I said. "Alan's gone missing on a canoe trip."

"Oh my god! What happened?"

"We're not totally sure. John was with him and got out in time. So did his dog. Alan went over the Cariboo Falls. They're eighty feet high and very rocky. John went crazy looking for him but couldn't find any trace. This was all yesterday afternoon."

"And why were they canoeing there? Didn't they know where they were?"

"Apparently not. John says they thought they were downstream of the falls all the time."

"Geez, that's unbelievable. Is there a search party?"

"Yeah, there is. They've started already. We're hopeful but don't know anything yet. But Ben, there's more to it."

"I'm sure there is. I'm betting it's not good."

"I've got a lot of very emotional actors on my hands. I'm not sure how to handle this and at least keep the other show going."

"Try to keep things positive and give them hope about the search party. Put the second show on double duty for as long as possible. Meanwhile, I'll get started on trying to find a substitute actor for Alan so we can get that show moving again."

Nowadays, tragedies merit grief counsellors who come to organizations, companies, schools. No such luck at the edge of the wilderness. We became each other's grief counsellors. We searched for answers to the unanswerable. And so the process began. It began with the questions.

The first one was why. Why Alan? Why at his age? Why now, in the middle of the season when things were going so well? Why here?

The next was who. Who is to blame? Who should bear the guilt? Was it John? Was it me for not controlling them more? After all, they were my employees. Indeed, I did have a short period of feeling some blame but realized that my control was only within the bounds of the theatre and what they did there. I could not possibly control their leisure time.

We all struggled with these for one of the most difficult weeks of everyone's lives. Perhaps in doing so, through endless tears and discussions, everyone found a new inner strength.

The second of our plays, a light musical comedy, continued and filled in most of the gaps where the first play should have been. In the meantime, Ben had found a new actor, Stephen, to take Alan's part. The play's director was again brought in, rehearsals accomplished, and the show was back "on the boards" within a week of Alan's disappearance. Ben had chosen well. To Stephen's everlasting credit, he had the good sense to know the difference between replacing Alan the actor and Alan the person.

About three weeks later, Alan's body was found by hikers well downriver from the falls. As they say, the discovery brought "closure." But what is closure? Is it real? Is it a convenient end to painful memories, to fearful anticipation, to guilt? Is it a signal that grieving is no longer relevant? Can we just slap our hands together and say, "OK, that's done. Now let's get on with our own important lives?"

For a tightly woven family of actors clinging to each other for emotional survival away from loved ones, the answers were all clearly no. For us, there was still a gaping hole in the middle of that family. Only time, that ageless prison, would eventually heal our wounds when our sentences were complete.

We still trudged daily up Main Street to the theatre, doffing hats to tourists and friends, warmly greeting them with a "Nice to see you, ma'am" and "How are you, pastor?" and "I see you've struck some pay dirt, Mr. Cameron." The brisk air still carried a mélange of coal smoke from George's blacksmith fire and pine scent from the forested hillsides. The tantalizing aroma of baking sourdough still beckoned Kelly, who had been adopted by John, but there was still no Alan to trade his rubbery face for a child's admiring glance. The hole remained. Although a warm August brought record numbers of tourists and our plays thrived, the success was bittersweet.

A day before we returned to the coast, I paid a visit to the Barkerville Cemetery, a small patch of overgrown fenced hillside under pine trees just outside town. In it was a collection of weather-beaten wooden grave markers in various stages of decay. Upon inspection, it soon became obvious that a majority of these belonged to miners and adventurers in their twenties and thirties who had succumbed to accidents—falls down mine shafts, exposure, disease—their dreams shattered. Like Alan, they were victims of the unforgiving frontier existence.

A waning summer breeze rustled the tall grass and seemed to whisper Alan's name as I stood amongst the graves. He was a dreamer too, an actor who wanted to be a playwright. He had come here to seek success. In fact, we were *all* dreamers, our company of humble thespians, seeking fortune and maybe fame from the thousands of tourists who now brought gold *into* town. Our company even made a modest profit for the season, our share of the golden dream. As for the miners of a century before, though, it did not come without a price.

Chapter Eight

Seven Deadly Sins

Our clients were primarily corporations, non-profit entities, government organizations, hotels, and the individuals who represented them. Most of the events for which we provided entertainment were out of the public spotlight. They were dinners, award ceremonies, conference sessions and openings, product launches, incentive evenings for top salespersons, dances, fundraisers, and social events, usually with hundreds or thousands of people in attendance. They were held in every kind of exotic locale: private homes, arenas, stadia, stores and malls, offices, farmers' fields, mountaintops, ferries and ships, trains, buses, ballrooms, private clubs, restaurants, midways, and assorted others.

Our encounters with these clients and their unusual needs demonstrated how the seven deadly sins of human nature could manifest themselves in surprisingly unpredictable forms.

* * *

A popular act with visitors to Canada—particularly male visitors—at conference dinners was a troupe of twenty-four teenage female dancers who were attired in tight red swimsuit-style tops with white belts, flesh-coloured long stockings, long white boots, elbow-length white gloves, and white, broad-brimmed hats. They performed a "Mountie" routine of precision choreography to the music of "The Maple Leaf Forever."

They had just arrived at the conference centre for their after-dinner performance one evening, and I was escorting them and their director-choreographer, Betty, to their green room. It was upstairs from the ballroom where they were to perform.

"OK, Betty, this is the place. It's a large room and we've given you lots of chairs, mirrors, tables, and coat racks with hangers. Also some coffee, soft drinks, and cookies. Let me know if there's anything else you need."

"It's perfect," she said. "We'll be fine."

"Oh, yes, it's also lockable, so the girls can leave valuables when they come downstairs."

"Thanks."

About an hour later I came to escort the dancers to the ballroom. I dutifully locked the door and proceeded downstairs with them. The show went off well and the thousand-strong audience gave the dancers a hearty round of applause. I watched from near one of the ballroom doors with Betty, and after the performance we retraced our steps in escorting the dancers back to the green room. I called security to have them open the door.

The first girls inside walked over to the coat racks while starting to strip off gloves and hats.

"Oh my god!" one of them shouted. "My underwear's gone."

"Mine too."

"And mine."

Not a stitch of undergarments was to be found.

"Check all your bags, girls," Betty said. "Make sure you still have wallets and money."

"Yup, it's all there."

"Nothing missing."

"Yeah, I'm OK."

Lingerie—somebody had a thing for lingerie. But who?

"I thought you said everything would be safe." Betty was upset.

"It was supposed to be," I said. "Conference centre security told me that once the door was locked it would be fine. I double-checked the door when we all left."

We reported the theft to security and to the client but nothing was ever recovered. I never knew if the perpetrator was a member of the client's group or conference centre staff, but someone added twenty-four new pieces to his perversely exotic collection that night.

* * *

"Fifties Themes" were among our most requested events. For some reason, the nostalgia of a perceived less-hectic era resonated with people. We would bring in immaculately preserved Ford Fairlanes, Corvettes, and Buicks, as well as Elvis lookalikes, original jukeboxes, and 50s-attired hostesses. An Asian client wanted all this and more for fifteen hundred top insurance salesmen holding a big dinner party in a hotel ballroom. He was especially adamant about one request.

"Everyone wants Playboy bunnies," he said. "All the salesmen are middle-aged and they remember the great times they had at Playboy clubs."

"Sure, no problem," I assured him. "What do you want them to do?"

"We're going to give them Polaroid cameras and they can go around taking pictures of the guests."

"Sounds easy. I'll make sure we get some attractive, friendly girls for you."

"And we want a really good rock and roll band."

"Will do. We have lots."

He neglected a vital point. There were to be no spouses accompanying the male guests.

The time came and the guests loved the cars, the dinner—hot dogs, sodas, popcorn, hamburgers, beer—and the band. The idea was that after dinner there would be only a short time until they left, since dancing was more or less out of the question without spouses. Unfortunately, they *really* loved the beer and the girls and wanted to hang around longer. Polaroid cameras were clicking madly as the bunnies took photos of groups of guests in a myriad of strange poses. Very soon things took a new twist as the guests began to photograph themselves with the girls.

One of the girls approached me.

"Someone pinched my ass."

Soon another one came over. "Some guy grabbed my butt when I was turned the other way."

And another one. "This idiot put his hand on my boobs but I slapped him away. Then he asked me up to his room."

"Doug, you've gotta do something. Now they want to dance with us."

"Maybe it's a cultural thing," I said, trying to calm the situation. "Try being forceful with them and don't give them the cameras. Your job's just to take pictures, nothing else."

It didn't work. And I couldn't just charge my client with harassment. I had to call a halt. He ended the event and sent the guests home to their hotel rooms.

I made a note to myself: not every culture in the world operates on the same moral wavelength.

* * *

Immorality and lust cross all social strata equally. However, there is only one class of people whose pride and sense of entitlement demand an environment befitting their stature.

I found this out one September when seventy presidents of the world's largest corporations visited Vancouver for private meetings. My company was fortunate enough to win the contract for their entertainment. It was exclusive stuff. Very high end. And they knew what they wanted. The setting for one event, though, was at odds with their standards. I made a preliminary visit to the venue with the organizer, accompanied by my decorator and designer, Lesley, and a private caterer he had also hired.

It was what could be called a "low end" hotel, but he liked the physical setting, surrounded by water. We were to create an old Parisian theme from the artistic halcyon days of the 1920s. The trouble was that the dinner and dance were to be held in the hotel's dining room and bar, a location that in everyday use was known locally as a "meat market." The thought crossed my mind that this was probably not far from what most such venues were like in Paris at the time we were trying to recreate. However, he had other ideas. As we walked around, he noted the required changes.

"OK, we're going to have to cover up these entrance walls," he said. "They're just too grubby."

"I've got an idea," Lesley said. "We can make a false-fronted Paris street to line them. We'll customize it for a perfect fit so the hotel walls won't be seen at all."

"Love it," he said.

We arrived at the end of the dining room where the band would be playing. It was surrounded by floor-to-ceiling glass with a small alcove in the middle.

"This section is ideal for the band, but it's too small. Why don't we knock out all the windows and we'll put the band just outside under a tent or temporary cover, and then the day after, we'll come back in and replace the glass?"

I wondered if he was serious. "Um, we can do that, but it will be really expensive. Let me see if I can get my stage guys to construct a custom stage to fit into the alcove. It will keep it more intimate and cost a lot less."

"Maybe. Get back to me. Money's not an issue."

Nice. We moved on to the kitchen.

"Oh, this is bad. Absolutely unacceptable. This will need to be gutted and cleaned from top to bottom. Bring in your own cooking machinery," he said to the caterer. "And don't forget, we won't be using any of the hotel's catering staff."

"Done," she said.

On to the washrooms.

At the entrance to both he gasped. The sinks were cracked and brown with dirt, the faucets rusty and dripping. Condom machines hung above the men's urinals.

He looked at Lesley and me. "Do people really live with this filth?"

"Apparently they do," I said.

"Well, we just can't leave them like this. Make sure all the washrooms are cleaned thoroughly. Replace all the sinks, faucets, and towel dispensers."

"No problem," Lesley said.

"We also have to do something about the condom machines. Our people can't see them hanging around."

Lesley's face lit up. "I know. We can cover them with old Parisian paintings of the era, maybe Chagall, Masson, and such."

"Great idea. Do it."

On the evening of the event, patrons on the way to their *affaires de la coeur* were politely told by four bricks of men in sunglasses that the hotel was temporarily closed as it had been "bought out" for a private grand soiree.

Alas, we had sanitized Paris. Gone was the gritty underbelly of the city with its sooted buildings and cracked paint. No sign lingered of an *Irma la Douce* waiting on a lamplit street corner for her lover, condom in hand.

Who but the vainglorious would try to make over the City of Light?

* * *

Silly me. I believed company presidents would know how to conduct business properly. I believed they would know a lot about accounting. I even believed they would be industrious and responsible. My naïveté caught up with me when planning for a national corporate meeting in Victoria.

After a site visit and a rewritten proposal, the company's president and I concluded negotiations for a British Pub Night. We were to provide an old bar, a Pearly Kings Trio, a Queen Elizabeth lookalike, darts, sidewalk chalk artists, fake double-decker bus, murals, and various and sundry props. It was going to be worth a nice amount for my company. I duly sent him a contract and then forgot about everything until a few days before the event when it was time to get ready.

The event was on a Monday, and on the Thursday before, I was checking our contracts and noticed something amiss. My client was in Ontario. I called him from our Vancouver office.

"Sorry to bother you, Dave, but I just noticed we don't have a signed contract from you or any deposit for the event on Monday. I'm worried. Is everything all right?"

"Yes, it's fine. I only operate on a handshake."

What a jerk! In this day and age. I couldn't believe it.

"I find that difficult, I'm afraid," I said. "How will I know if you're going to accept our performers or the decorations we agreed on?"

"Guess you'll just have to trust me. If I like it, you'll get paid. If not, you won't."

Now I was getting really incensed. Should I risk going ahead or cancel and be out the advances I'd already paid suppliers? I took a chance.

"OK, at the very least I'll need the deposit I requested in the written contract."

"Fine." He sounded annoyed. "I'll have it couriered to you tomorrow."

"That's a good start. Any chance you'll change your mind about signing that contract?"

"Nope, sorry. I'll see you in Victoria on Monday."

Now I was committed—and more worried. I decided to make a credit check on my client through Dun and Bradstreet. He was loaded and could have bought me out many times over. That was a good sign.

In spite of it, Monday was a day of anxiety. I kept wondering if he would find some little thing wrong and tell me it was not what we agreed on. How could I refute that kind of statement without a signed contract? I knew from experience that small claims of this magnitude almost never got settled, even if you won with a favourable court decision. No doubt he also knew it and hence never signed contracts. Luckily nothing was wrong and we were paid within a week.

I vowed to never work with an individual like this again.

His sin? Fiscal and ethical torpor.

* * *

In the late 1950s and into the 1960s, after a short-lived fad of telephone booth stuffing, students around the world decided it would be more fun to stuff themselves into Volkswagen Beetles. I think the record was eighteen people in the mid-60s—*and* with doors and windows closed and no body parts sticking out, one of the "rules."

In the late 90s we got a request for VW stuffing. The event, once again, was a 50s theme.

My client, the event organizer for this dinner meeting of a national shoe company, was clear. "We want to have three perfectly preserved old cars for photo opps and also a VW Beetle. We're going to have a contest to see how many people we can stuff into the bug. I know it's been eclipsed, but we want to see if we can beat the original record from the 60s."

"It may be hard to find one," I said. "Most people who have well-preserved vintage cars are pretty loathe to even let anyone *touch* them, let alone *stuff* them."

"I promise we'll be very careful—no shoes allowed, no sharp objects, no drinks or food inside or around the cars, especially for the Beetle."

"OK. Do you have insurance to cover damage, just in case?"

"Yes, absolutely."

"Let me see what I can do."

I found three mint classic vehicles for the photo opps: an orange and white Plymouth, a red Ford Thunderbird convertible, and a black DeSoto. As expected, it was harder to locate a good VW whose owner would let it be used for stuffing, but one finally surfaced. He made me swear that we would guard it with our lives. When he drove it into the convention centre ballroom for the event, I realized why. Immaculately preserved, it was a baby blue '69 Bug, highly polished and with not a scratch or even a fingerprint on it.

"I usually like to stay for these events," he said, "but I have another engagement. Just make sure you take good care of it. I'll pick it up later tonight after the event."

"Don't worry, it's in good hands."

After dinner, it was time for the VW Stuffing contest. The organizer divided up the guests into three teams: Team Loafers, Team Sneakers, and Team Sandals. After fifteen minutes or so for each team to survey the space available and determine roughly who would fit where, Team Loafers started things off. Doffing watches, shoes, belts, and anything that protruded or took up useless space, they managed to cram fourteen bodies into the little bug. Twenty minutes later, they emerged sweating amidst a tirade of one-liners about farts, smelly feet, and lack of deodorant.

Team Sneakers went next. Judging by the number of members under five feet six, it looked like there was a good chance they would surpass Team Loafers. The shortest members went first. Then the team handlers pushed the larger ones onto the top of the seats and stretched them out along the inside of the roofline. Good planning. They managed to get eighteen, equalling the original record.

I told them to take a time out while I checked the car. It was still in perfect shape although a tad malodorous on the inside, nothing that a good air freshener couldn't fix. "OK, you can load the last team," I said.

Team Sandals was ready and pumped. They even had a team cheer. There was nobody over five feet four inches tall. The girls all looked like gymnasts and half the guys looked like jockeys. They were ready for the challenge. In an amazing example of suppleness, the most petite girl squeezed her lower half *under* the brake pedal and upper half around the inside of the gearshift. One of the jockey-types, a fellow named Marv, almost mirrored the move on the passenger side. They kept the layers coming, piling on top of these two. It must have been excruciatingly uncomfortable at the bottom, but with a couple of more layers, all we could hear on the outside were muffled groans. Finally, after reaching eighteen, there was still room just near the passenger door for one more if only the door would close. They had taken slightly longer to reach eighteen than the last team, so the extra person was absolutely necessary if they were to win. It was another girl. She could only fit half sideways, which meant her shoulder butted up against the passenger door. The door clicked half shut but not fully. The guys outside pushed the door. The girl screamed. Nineteen was not meant to be. They unloaded, dejected. A few swore. Finally, Marv made it out. He was sweating and angry.

"Sonuvabitch!" he shouted, as he put his shoes back on. "Half an hour of pain and we don't make it. What the hell happened? Fucking car! The door should have closed better."

I watched from a few yards away. Well, he's mad, that's to be expected.

Before I knew what was happening, he leapt onto the bug's hood, then onto the roof, and proceeded to jump up and down. I could hear the metal crunching.

Four of his friends grabbed his left arm and leg and yanked him off the roof. It was too late. The beetle was squished—and I was going to be in big trouble.

My client rushed over to me and immediately apologized. "We'll pay for the damages, whatever they cost."

"Thank you," I said. "The hard part is going to be telling the owner."

And it was, but fortunately he accepted the apology and settlement graciously.

Wrath. It always hurts. You just never know how and when it will strike.

* * *

A wealthy real estate mogul hired us to decorate his fortieth birthday party at a local hotel.

"It has to be spectacular," he said, "lots of flowers and Greek columns, you know, a classical theme. My wife likes that."

My decorator, Lesley, designed the event, trying hard to get the exact concept my client wanted. She brought in beautiful Doric columns, faux marble arches, and classical urns filled to overflowing with ivy, grapes, vines, and assorted florals. She matched all the colours and coordinated room décor with the buffets. Just as she was finishing setting it all up, I noticed my client surveying the scene.

"How do you like it?" I asked.

"It looks fabulous, doesn't it, honey?"

"Absolutely wonderful," said his wife.

It was so impressive I decided to record it all with a series of my own photos.

The day after the event, I called the client to see if everything had gone well. He wasn't in—and he didn't call back. Not unusual, I thought. I sent our invoice for the remainder of the money he owed us.

Two weeks went by. Nothing.

A couple of more calls and a couple of more weeks. Nothing.

A few increasingly nasty e-mails accompanying copies of the invoice. Two more weeks. Nothing.

After about two months, I finally connected with a phone call. I asked my client where the money was.

"It's not coming," he said. "We didn't like what you did."

"You told me it was fabulous right before the event. What's the problem?"

"We decided it wasn't. Sorry. No money."

I realized there was nothing to be gained by arguing over the phone. It was time for more drastic action. This man was obviously as arrogant as they came.

I decided to take my problem to small claims court since it was a relatively small amount and small claims was a lot cheaper than hiring a lawyer. I had never been inside a courtroom before. It was a brand new experience, but I was certain I was in the right and would soon see my money. Boy, was I naïve.

It took three more months before a court date. My client managed to squeeze out of that date with a story about hardship in being available. That delayed the next date for another three months. Then there was a court-caused delay. The final appearance for settlement was over a year after the event. By now, the interest owing by my client was almost as much as the original invoice.

He never showed up in court. His lawyer offered a lame reason and the judge awarded in my favour. There really was no contest. Great, I thought, that's the end of my problems with this guy.

In a perfect world, the story would end there. I would go away with all my money and everything would be right again. Unfortunately, not in the real world.

It became apparent that my client was accustomed to avoiding the law. He knew every trick. Change bank accounts. Keep one step ahead. Never put all your money in once place. Even with a court judgment against you.

To collect on the judgment for this small amount of money, I would have to eventually hire a bailiff and track down my constantly evasive client in order to serve him and collect enough of his assets to sell and get my payment. This was a risky move and not worth it for the amount of cash. It could very well end up costing me a whole lot more. I decided to eat the loss.

A year later I read in the local paper that a number of other companies were owed money by this man, most in the hundreds of thousands of dollars. In a warped way, I felt comforted to know I was not alone.

I learned immensely from the experience. Not the least lesson was that greed can take eccentric forms. Not wanting to pay a fair price for service is just one of them.

I also knew in my heart that my client would eventually pay the price for his greed.

* * *

A gangly lady with a green dress, short-cropped brown hair, and an excess of gold bling, Mrs. Edna Schwartz announced herself and poked her head just inside the door to the dining room. She beckoned me over.

"Who's this for?" she asked.

"Bradley Krebs," I replied. "It's his Bar Mitzvah tonight."

"Oh, it doesn't look very good, not like Gordon Paley's last month. He had a big Wild West theme. He loves cowboys, you know. There were live horses to ride outside, real cactus inside. Oh, and they even had trick roping. I just love to see what everyone does."

Edna was a wee bit premature in her judgment.

The room behind me was in total disarray: the floor was covered with camouflage netting, artificial plants and greenery were strewn everywhere, stalks of bamboo were propped against the walls, tables and chairs were askew.

"Well, we just started decorating," I said. "If you come back in about four hours, you'll see a big difference."

"Yes, I will, definitely. I'm planning my daughter's Bat Mitzvah and I can get lots of ideas." She turned and set out for the bar with a determined step, gold earrings jangling up and down.

We were in the throes of transforming the snobbish golf club's dining room into the heart of deepest, darkest Africa. It was a popular venue for the Bar Mitzvah set. My client, Mrs. Debbie Krebs, was insistent that this was to be an event that would set the standard for all others. Her son, Bradley, was crazy about wild animals and Africa. She was not reticent in spending on him. The bill was going to be well into five figures. We brought in jungle growth that would make Livingstone and Stanley proud: palm trees and bushes lined the walls, vines hung from the ceiling over all the tables, life-sized stuffed gorillas and rhinos poked through the foliage, pygmies held a meeting in a thatched hut. There was even a replica of the Jungle Queen river boat for the DJ to broadcast from.

At five in the afternoon, Edna returned and teetered into the middle of the room.

"Oh, this is wonderful. You were right," she said to me. "What a difference. This is better than Gordon's."

"Thank you. Glad you like it."

She spotted my client a few feet away and walked over to her, gushing, "Debbie, Debbie. This is soooo good. Bradley's going to love it." They were still within earshot.

"Do you think so?" my client said. "I really hope he does. God knows, I wanted to do it right after seeing Lisa Paley's setup last month. There was just no way it was not going to be as good."

"Well, it is."

"Thanks. By the way, did you know Frank and I have split up?"

"No, I didn't."

"It was a couple of weeks ago, just when we were beginning to plan for this."

"I'm so sorry." The words didn't quite match the lack of sympathy on Edna's face.

"Well, don't be," my client said. "He's paying for all this but he doesn't know it yet. I just spend and send him the invoices."

I couldn't believe what I was hearing, but then I guess some people lived different lives than I was used to.

As a wise man once said, "Envy eats nothing but its own heart."

* * *

Hearty meals were common for the clients we served. Feasts, however, those sumptuous demonstrations of gustatory nirvana, were rare. No wonder. They were expensive. An aperitif and four or five different wines all had to be paired perfectly with six to eight meal courses. Not only were they expensive, they took a long time to prepare *and* to eat. We provided entertainment at a handful of such feasts. One was unforgettable—for all the wrong reasons.

Michelle, one of my regular clients, was easygoing and amiable. She didn't, as they say, "sweat the small stuff." Her company was known as a PCO or professional conference organizer. They brought into town conferences with hundreds and often thousands of attendees. These conferences were worth a lot of money to the city. She called me up with a big request.

"Doug, I've got a conference for twelve hundred technical specialists who want a spectacular Canadian dinner show. The important thing is they need to be occupied during dinner. It's going to be six courses. You know, one of those long, obscenely extravagant things, two hundred bucks a plate. What can you do?"

"How about an Indian legend acted out between dinner courses?"

"Sounds perfect. Can you write it up and I'll take it to them?"

A week or so later we received the group's reply. They loved it. Full steam ahead.

I set about organizing the details. It was a Cirque du Soleil–type show that combined aerial acrobats, native dancers, contortionists, a magician, and fire performers. The story would be told in short segments between dinner courses using these performers in various combinations.

The finale would be an aerial silk performance by the acrobats at the end of dinner.

Event day arrived. Dining tables were weighed down with six courses worth of flatware and stemware. The stage was set. Sound checks were complete. Adrenalin was surging.

An aperitif commenced the proceedings.

As soon as the *amuse-bouche* was served, the show began with a magician and some hand-held fire.

Between soup and salad, native dancers, one in an impressive six-foot-long raven mask, got into the legend. By now, the aperitif had been consumed and the first Pinot Grigio was being poured to go with the upcoming salmon.

After the fish came contortionists writhing around the stage as animals and birds. Copious wine refills were dispensed. The room's white noise edged up a few decibels. Things were going well.

A filet mignon entrée and two refills of Australian Shiraz made it difficult to talk to anyone farther than a foot away. I half wondered if buns might be flying soon. Fortunately, our fire performer came next and temporarily silenced the assembly as she traced fiery arcs with twirling fire poi.

As the poi slowly sputtered out, the wait staff cleared dishes and loaded up the only remaining stemware with Okanagan ice wine.

Guests were into the giddy stage. Pockets of laughter bounced around the room like out-of-control ping pong balls. The occasional cackly scream told me that this was about the limit to guests' endurance. It was time for the finale.

After a scrumptious-looking cheesecake came the aerial acrobats or "silk artists." The cackles and ping-ponging laughter ceased. They were replaced by gasps as the artists spun and unravelled twenty feet in the air. They finished to prolonged applause, dropping gracefully from their red silks that now hung almost to the ground.

Michelle was smiling. She raised a glass of wine to me. "Thanks, Doug. Well done. Come and join us for a glass."

"I will. Just let me go backstage first and thank the performers." I figured it would be OK to have a drink since the event was over and guests would quickly be leaving the room.

The performers were all in a joyous mood, still buzzing from their well-deserved ovations. I gave them their cheques and thanked them. I hadn't been there for more than two minutes when I heard shouts and cheers from out front, which was blocked from my view by a tall, black stage curtain. One of my stage managers suddenly appeared. She was frantic.

"Doug, you've gotta come back out. Two guys are climbing the silks!"

"What? I thought everyone was supposed to leave. The event's over."

"No," she said. "They've kept the bars open. People are staying and drinking. I think these guys are pretty far gone."

"Crap! Like they didn't have enough booze already!"

I rushed back out front. Sure enough, two young guests were making their way up the silks, each about twenty-five feet high. A female security official was trying desperately to get them down. She was short and far too sweet for her line of work—she would have had trouble wrestling a Chihuahua into submission. She was standing beside one silk and, as I reached it, had somehow, miraculously, convinced Idiot #1 to come down. He probably succumbed to the sight of the uniform rather than her unintimidating commands.

"Stay here and make sure nobody else tries this," I said to her.

Then I looked over at the other silk. It was about thirty feet away. No security person. My heart skipped a beat. Idiot #2 was already around twenty feet up the silk and still climbing, to the encouraging shouts of his friends on the ground. Just as I arrived, he decided to hang upside down. I had a sinking feeling in the pit of my stomach. Visions of endless rounds of litigation by a quadriplegic in a wheelchair, designed to divest me of all my savings—not to mention the assets of Michelle's company—rushed ominously through my head. I lost it.

Shaking the silk, I screamed at him. "Come down, you fucking jerkoff!"

At that moment, the artist who owned the silks arrived. "Don't shake it," he said. "It may make him fall."

"OK, what do we do?"

"Just wait. He'll get tired and come down."

And he did.

As his feet touched the ground, I unleashed a volley of expletives at him.

"What's wrong with you? Do you have a death wish? You could have been severely injured, not to mention costing all of us a lot of money. You're a fucking idiot!" His nose had a bull's eye on it.

By now a large crowd had gathered around us. Michelle pushed her way over to me and grabbed my arm in the backswing.

"Wow, I've never seen you like this. It's OK," she said, trying to calm me. "He's safe and nothing happened."

"Well, it could have." My blood pressure slowly returned to normal. "What the hell was that—and why did they do it?"

A guest volunteered some information.

"I was sitting at their table," she said. "They're students from the engineering faculty at UBC. They were betting each other who could climb up the silks first and touch the top. They had way too much booze."

I found it quite amazing how gluttony manifested itself.

Dante would have loved my clients.

Chapter Nine

Celebrities

Although our company dealt mainly with entertainers who could be termed journeymen—very skilled, but not well-known—we occasionally worked with others who were celebrities. These were people who either were or would become household names. Sometimes we actually worked directly with the celebrities, sometimes only around the periphery of their auras. The experiences were almost always memorable.

* * *

Like most boomers, I was a fan of rock and roll from the time I was a kid growing up in the late 50s and early 60s, about the same time as many legends began their careers. Among these were the Everly Brothers. I bought their first recordings as soon as they came out on 45s, including "Bye, Bye Love," "Wake Up, Little Susie," and "All I Have to Do Is Dream." Today, the first two bars of any of those songs bring back memories of warm summer evenings, vivid green and red cars with outlandish tailfins, and the smell of bubble gum and leather baseball mitts. The Everlys were fixed in my past.

Pretty well all of us in a certain age bracket also remember where we were when two great historical events occurred in the 1960s. On November 22, 1963, I was in a high school classroom when a radio voice first announced the assassination of President John F. Kennedy. On July 20, 1969, I and the world watched our black and white TVs, transfixed as that same emotionally charged voice formed the background to a grainy film of astronaut Neil Armstrong stepping onto the surface of the moon. These events propelled Walter Cronkite into the spotlight as a famous news anchor, so much so that he was often cited as "the most trusted man in America."

Just short of a decade later, I fell in love with Crystal Gayle when I watched her perform "Don't It Make My Brown Eyes Blue" on TV. Her long hair, svelte body, and near-perfect face were irresistible for any normal male. To prove the point, she was later voted one of the fifty most beautiful people in the world.

These were talented people.

World-class celebrities.

In 1987, a prestigious client of ours brought all of them to a high-powered incentive meeting in Vancouver to entertain the top North American salesmen of a well-known computer company. During the four-day meeting, we got to literally rub shoulders with the celebs and, as I recall, exchange some pleasantries. I admit even now to being slightly awestruck. We also watched them perform. They did admirably, singing all their hits, and for Walter, acting as MC. They all received nice applause. No doubt they had cost a lot of money.

Our job for this client, however, was much smaller. We were to arrange an outdoor barbecue lunch for the salesmen and their spouses, including a stage show. It was to be on the last day of their time in Vancouver, after all the celebrities had performed. Ben and I were more than a little concerned.

"How the hell can we compete with all this star power?" Ben asked when, weeks before, we were beginning to plan the show. "We're the last thing on the menu and it has to be good."

"Say, isn't this the twentieth anniversary of the Sgt. Pepper album release?" I offered.

"Yeah, so what good is that?"

"Suppose we did some kind of musical tribute?"

"It just might work." Ben agreed—not something he was good at. "All the guests should be able to relate to the Beatles."

We called up one of our best bands for a meeting. Their name was Visibly Shakin', a somewhat premature expectation of their audiences' reactions. But in our experience, they did deliver on that expectation. The leader's name was Dave.

"Can you put together an hour-long anniversary show about the Sgt. Pepper album?" Ben asked.

"Are you kidding? What a coincidence!" Dave said. "We were actually just thinking of doing that this year. We'll get the girls doing some cute stuff with 'Lovely Rita' and 'Lucy in the Sky.'" They had two gorgeous lead singers.

"And we'll bring in the Colormen."

Ben and I looked at each other.

"Who are the Colormen?" we both asked, almost at once. We didn't like to put unknowns onstage without testing audience reactions.

"Awesome, awesome group. Four guys. They sing a cappella, perform choreographed dance routines, and they're funny. Kind of like the Nylons on speed mixed with the Jackson Five."

"OK," Ben said reluctantly. "Give it a try, but we want to see a rehearsal first."

Trust can be a beautiful thing, if and when it works. We took a chance.

The final day of the conference approached rapidly—too rapidly. Life in entertainment is always hectic, so we didn't actually see the rehearsal until two hours before the real show. Now the trust thing turned into anxiety. In special events, unlike theatre, there's only one chance to get it right. Dave had delivered before and the rehearsal was good, but was it good enough for this group of jaded salesmen who had already seen the best of the best?

The noon sun of mid-June reflected off the nearby water and beamed down on the outdoor stage, a perfect Vancouver setting. At least we had that going for us. The smell of barbecuing ribs and sea air added to the enticing environment. The guests were in high spirits.

Then it was time for the show.

We knew from the first note that Dave and his group had the audience hooked. It was obviously the right music for the right crowd on the right day. The previously unknown Colormen became instant hits. Well before the finale, the crowd was standing and applauding and stayed that way for the last ten minutes of the show, dancing, singing, and jumping in time to the famous songs. It was one of those moments when you thank God or your lucky stars for good fortune.

Years after, our client continued to tell us that his guests liked to reminisce and tell him how much better our humble, hour-long musical review was compared to the star power of the Everly Brothers, Crystal Gayle, and Walter Cronkite that they had seen for three days. It just proved that small can be beautiful, and that trust *can* work.

* * *

Before we added entertainers to our talent roster, we always sought to either interview them or, ideally, listen to a tape or CD or watch them perform. One type of performer never in short supply was pianists.

The young female on the other end of the phone sounded like she was still in high school.

"Hello, Mr. Matthews?"

"Yes, this is Doug Matthews."

"Hi, I'm a pianist and vocalist just new in town and I'm looking for some work in lounges. Can I come down to see you?"

We booked a few hotel lounges, typically evening gigs that required a friendly personality, a large repertoire of songs, a strong voice, and if female, a high rating on the attractiveness scale. Good legs didn't hurt. Often, musical ability took second place. It sounded as if she might fit.

"Sure. Come on down. I have an opening tomorrow at 10:00 a.m. Can you make it?"

"Yes, I'll be there. Thanks."

At the appointed time, Kathy ushered in a petite, cute blonde in a short dress. She was twenty, twenty-one at the most. Ben and I greeted her. She sat in front of Ben's desk and crossed her legs. She was nervous but managed to keep poised.

"Glad you could make it. We have a few questions we need to ask," Ben said. He was never one for preliminaries.

"And we'd also like to see your promo kit and a tape if you have one," I added.

Ben dutifully started going through our sheet of questions—name, address, phone, hours you want to work, etc., and then we chatted a bit.

"I see you're from Nanaimo," I said. This was a small town on Vancouver Island, an hour and a half by ocean-going ferry from the big city. "Why did you come to Vancouver?"

"I want to make a name for myself, and it's pretty hard in Nanaimo." She leaned across the desk and dropped a small cassette tape onto her promo kit. "Here's my demo."

"OK, fair enough," I said. "We do have a couple of lounges that we book. We'll listen to your tape and try to fit you in if we like what we hear."

"I think you will," she said, with an alluring, fresh-faced smile. "I've had some pretty good teachers and a lot of favourable reviews of my school concerts." Whatever nervousness she came in with had been replaced by a latent confidence. She had more going for her than we were used to in a casual pianist.

I could see Ben getting antsy. He made no bones from the outset of our partnership that time was money and interviews should never be longer than ten minutes. We were at that point.

"Thanks a lot," she said. Her voice really was sweet—and sultry—perfect for lounges. "I hope you like my music."

As she got up and left the office, I watched Ben eyeing the shapely legs.

"It's like giving a squirrel nuts when he's got no teeth," he said under his breath, one of his favourite quotes whenever an attractive performer presented herself. I was sure she must have heard him, but she kept walking.

Her tape was very good. "Wave" by Antonio Carlos Jobim and "42nd Street" by Harry Warren were beautifully rendered jazz classics that demonstrated a musical maturity beyond her years. There was no question she would easily fit the bill for some of our lounge work, so we put her on the top of our crowded roster of singers and pianists. Unfortunately, this work didn't materialize immediately, but two months later, an opening did come up for a month-long gig. I thought of the petite blonde and called her.

Her mother answered.

"Sorry, she's gone to Los Angeles."

"Is she coming back soon?"

"No, I think she'll probably be staying down there."

"Too bad. I had a gig for her."

She never came back.

Diana Krall had slipped through our fingers.

* * *

One mark of a true professional is the ability to forge ahead in spite of adversity. It's the "show must go on" mentality. Most celebrities have it. Certainly many that I worked with did.

Bobby Curtola was one. A Canadian teen idol of the early 60s, he first became famous for his hit "Fortune Teller" in 1962. He was—and still is—a consummate performer. But I didn't think so when I first met him in the late 80s.

"Hi, I'm Bobby Curtola." He rushed up to me with a grin as wide as Saskatchewan.

"Good to meet you, Bobby. I'm Doug." This is definitely not like most celebrities, I mused. Most are serious and almost always arrogant. He's way too friendly.

"So what's the gig all about tonight, Doug?" he asked, still smiling.

"It's for a national company, about a thousand people. You're the after-dinner entertainment."

"OK. That's cool." He was walking around checking out the green room, dressed in a leather jacket like the Fonz. He reminded me of a perennial teenager, still in high school. He was in his forties.

"Let's get the sound check out of the way," he said. "I want to tell you about this health drink we've got." This struck me as a little strange. Mind you, Bobby had been pushing drinks and various products since he became Coca-Cola's number one spokesman with his recording of "Things Go Better with Coke" in 1964.

His sound check went smoothly, his musical director leading the way through it for our audio engineer. Then we were back in the green room sitting around a table. His band was tuning, playing with their instruments, drinking coffee, and generally getting ready. Bobby didn't seem at all concerned about anything technical, a welcome change, I thought, from others who fretted for two hours over the smallest details of their microphones and monitors.

"Doug, I want you to take a look at this stuff," he said, pulling his chair over to show off a bottle of oddly coloured liquid. "It works magic, man. I am incredibly healthy thanks to this drink. It's got all kinds of natural vegetable juices and every vitamin and mineral you can imagine." His youthful exuberance was a tribute to this fact. However, his sales pitch continued and I didn't have the heart to stop him since he was so enthusiastic.

What's with this guy? I thought. Shouldn't he be at least a little more concerned about his imminent concert, since it's only half an hour away? Ah, well, different people get in the zone in different ways.

As we walked to the conference room where our guests were dining, Bobby continued to regale me with stories from his past, throwing in the occasional reminder about his drink. He wasn't at all worried about the show, at least not obviously. This was unusual. Most people—even vets—showed some nervousness.

"Oh, by the way," he said, "I come in from the back of the room." I thought he was just making the show up as he went along. Not good. We stopped at the room's entrance instead of going around the back to enter via the kitchen, the side where the stage was.

"What's the matter, Doug? You look nervous," he said with an even bigger grin than when we met. This isn't the way it should be, I thought. Things are reversed.

"No, I'm OK," I lied.

By now his band was onstage, all the way across the room. I heard his musical director announce his name and wondered how in hell he was going to get across the room in time for the first song. I opened the door, a spotlight hit him, and Bobby started singing. And there was that great big dimpled smile. He shimmied his way through a dozen or more tables, stopping every so often to serenade a guest, who would usually turn tomato red. He didn't miss a beat. Onstage he danced, joked, and sang all his hits, regularly visiting the audience and schmoozing with the ladies. They ate it up. Obviously, everything was planned.

Then, during one of his forays into the audience, I heard a tremendous thump and everything went dead—sound, lights, even the audience. The room was plunged into blackness. This *wasn't* planned.

But Bobby kept singing. No mic. No band. No follow-spot. He just kept on singing. He still hadn't missed a beat. He even continued to joke with the ladies as if nothing had happened.

Then his drummer picked up the beat. His guitarist found his acoustic guitar and began accompanying Bobby. All in total darkness.

Within a minute, the audience reacted. They weren't afraid of the dark; they were amazed by Bobby. They started screaming.

By the time the blown circuit breaker was reset about ten minutes later, it was organized chaos. I had never seen anything like it.

This guy was a pro with a capital P.

After the show I congratulated Bobby and thanked him for his professionalism.

"No problem, man," he said. "You know, you just learn to roll with the punches in this business. Now, about this drink …"

* * *

My mother adored Jimmie Rodgers. I knew because whenever "Honeycomb" or "Kisses Sweeter than Wine" came on our old Motorola cabinet radio, she would ask me to turn it up. Then she would pause from her laundry or cooking and gaze off into the distance.

"Doesn't he have a beautiful voice?" she'd say, "and he's *so* good looking." I imagined her thirty years younger as a screaming teenager at one of his concerts. She was past that but she certainly recognized the talent of the man. His incredible, smooth voice spanned three octaves—without using falsetto.

It was 1957 and Jimmie Rodgers's star was ascending—straight up. The two songs my mother liked were back-to-back hits. They were followed in short succession by several more. In the late 50s he was the most popular musical star in North America next to Elvis. He appeared on every major television variety show and with every major recording star. He toured the world. He was also in a number of movies. For the next ten years he continued to record, charting twenty-two gold records. Then the music stopped.

I didn't hear of him again until we hired him for a private corporate event at a posh Vancouver businessmen's club in the late 80s.

I picked him up at the airport. It wasn't hard to spot him. He still had dark, sparkling eyes, black pompadour-style hair, slightly bushy black eyebrows, and a rugged, handsome face. Not much seemed to have changed from his younger pictures.

"Hello, Mr. Rodgers?"

"Yeah, that's me."

"I'm Doug Matthews. I'll be escorting you around for the show and to your hotel."

"Please call me Jimmie. Wow, this is great. I didn't expect a welcome." He seemed humble for a man of such talent.

"We like to treat our performers well," I said. We retrieved his bags and guitar and walked to my car. As we drove downtown, we talked.

"I've been up here a few times, just for fishing holidays. I liked Vancouver from the moment I saw it," he said. "A beautiful city."

I wondered what he had been doing since his string of hits in the late 50s and early 60s. I broached the subject.

"You know, Jimmie, my mom just loved you. She couldn't get enough of your singing. I think you recorded last in 1967 or so. Is that right?"

"Yeah, that's right, but I had a little setback the same year. I was pulled over one night in LA by an off-duty cop. Apparently I'd made him mad, cut him off or something, although I don't remember doing anything like that. I rolled my window down and he hit me with something, maybe the butt of a gun. He yanked me out of the car and broke my arm. Then he kicked me, dragged me around in the mud, and beat me pretty bad."

"God, that's terrible," I said.

"I had three brain surgeries and my skull was reconstructed with a twenty-nine-square-inch metal plate that holds everything together."

"Holy shit! How's the singing?"

"I can't always hit the high notes anymore," he said with a wistful look.

I was almost speechless. "Well, we're really glad you could make it up here." The question was, Could he deliver for this show? Maybe he wasn't such a good choice. This affluent crowd was pretty picky about their entertainment. They could detect when someone didn't have it anymore.

"How long did it take you to get back doing shows?" I asked.

"Up until a couple of years ago. Long after the incident I had massive headaches, mood swings, loss of balance. At first I couldn't walk or talk or remember songs. It was a pretty rough time."

"I can imagine."

I checked him into his hotel, then we went over to the club for the rehearsal and show. We had hired a backup trio for him. Jimmie came with his music charts and handed them out to the musicians. Then I realized he very much had it together.

"OK, here's where the guitar solo is for one refrain … I come in right here, so don't be late … on this song we all end together after I move my arm like this … we need to transpose this song from G to F …" The entire rehearsal was exact. No questions left unanswered for the pickup band who, with other headliners, were often left scrambling with bits and pieces of charts and instructions. Jimmie was clearly a perfectionist.

The show went off without a hitch. The city's well-heeled fathers and their spouses were suitably impressed, they all being of the right age to remember Jimmie in his prime. They never noticed that "Oh-Oh, I'm Falling in Love Again" and "Secretly" had to be transposed down so Jimmie could hit the high notes. He had only mentioned the beating incident in passing, almost as if it was unimportant.

The next day I drove him back to the airport.

"My doctor said I would never walk again," he volunteered out of the blue. "But you know, I have a lot of faith in God and I was determined. I recently started jogging and I'm even thinking about skydiving. How about that?"

As we parted at the airport, I realized this was a man of passion and incredible inner strength. I was happy to have met him.

The next time I saw my mother I told her about Jimmie.

"You would have loved him, Mom. He sang all those songs you liked back in the 50s and he's just a really friendly, down-to-earth guy. He's still good-looking, too"

Her face lit up. "Oh, I wish I could have met him," she said, "but what a horrible thing to happen. I hope he'll be OK."

"Mom, I think he's going to be just fine."

Several years later, I read that at the age of fifty-four, Jimmie did in fact take up skydiving and at fifty-five he was studying the martial art Aikido. The metal plate was finally removed from his skull as the bone had miraculously healed naturally. He has written a book and screenplay about his life entitled *Dancing on the Moon*. He still performs. He is closing in on eighty.

* * *

Paul was a good friend who owned a recording studio and was well connected in the Vancouver music scene. We often worked together to create special songs for clients and traded new talent that we encountered. Usually we just gave each other the name and phone number of the talent. On one occasion it was different.

"Hey, Doug, I've got someone in the studio you should listen to." Paul was on the phone and he sounded breathless. "Can you come down this afternoon?"

"Sure. I'll be there in half an hour." What's the big deal? I wondered.

At the studio Paul introduced me to a fresh-faced kid of about nineteen accompanied by an older woman. The kid had purposely unkempt hair and a puppy dog face. He was dressed in casual slacks and a sports shirt, no jeans like most others his age. It helped him to look more mature. The woman was tall, her face stern. She reminded me of one of my stricter grade-school teachers.

We exchanged pleasantries, then Paul played back one of the kid's demo songs that he had recorded in the studio. It was a Sinatra tune. Everyone watched for my reaction as the music enveloped us.

I sat stunned, feeling the shivers doing a jig up and down my spine, and occasionally shaking my head in disbelief. The rich, smooth baritone was *better* than Sinatra, better than most crooners I had *ever* heard. When the song was over, all I could say was, "Wow!"

"I'm sorry. What did you say your name was again?"

"It's Michael. Michael Bublé," the kid answered with a confident smile.

"And I'm Michael's manager," said Bev, the woman accompanying him.

"Well, Michael and Bev, that's quite a voice. I have a feeling it's going to take you a long way, Michael," I said.

"Michael's just won the Canadian Youth Talent Search," Bev said, in affirmation.

"That's not surprising," I said.

"Paul tells me he really values your opinion, so he asked you to come down and hear this. Michael wants to perform live and also record, but we don't know what direction to take him."

"Well, my expertise isn't in recording," I replied, "but I may be able to help him with his stage presence and in performing live. I haven't seen him perform yet, so I don't know how much help he might need. What we usually do is put our newer performers onstage and test out audience reaction. If it's good we put them in bigger shows and perhaps find someone who can get them a record deal. Michael certainly has the singing chops. He probably just needs some more experience onstage."

"Yeah, I'd like to do that," Michael said.

I could see that Bev was not totally convinced. "He also doesn't want to do just Sinatra and the oldies. We don't want him labelled as an impersonator. There are enough people who do that." She made it clear who was in charge of his career.

"So, Michael, do you have any other songs in your repertoire, like rock or country—maybe some originals?" I asked. "You know, other stuff besides Sinatra?"

"Yeah, a few. I grew up in front of the radio listening to all my grandfather's old standards and tried to sing them, so I have them pretty much down. Also quite a few Elvis and Beatles songs."

"What about originals?"

"I never learned to play an instrument, so nothing now. I can only sing." Michael looked me straight in the eye. "Apart from playing hockey, I've only ever wanted to be a singer," he added. The look shouted determination.

"So what do you think?" Bev asked.

"It sounds like we should get him a good backup band and someone to work up a stage show using what he has to begin with," I said. "We have a really good guitarist named Henry who can take him under his wing and put a show together."

"OK, it's a start," said Bev.

"Yeah, that's cool. Let's do it," Michael agreed.

The next two or three months were spent putting a small show together, with our guitarist Henry rehearsing Michael and working on several jazz standards. He performed his first show for us for free just to try it out and test the audience reaction. It was a major fundraiser for a well-known local charity.

All the songs were note-perfect. I was impressed with Michael's confidence onstage. He had already perfected some patently original moves, alternating a naturally casual singing style with audience banter. This was a good start.

The audience reaction, though, was non-existent, pure apathy.

The only comment came from one of the well-off VIP guests. "Who the hell is this guy? He's got really stupid-looking hair." I never told Michael.

I was frustrated. OK, so that didn't work out as I had expected. Yet it was so typical of haughty wealth. I should have known; I had seen it before. Their only recognition of talent came when they had to pay half a million or more for it. Even then it was a begrudging recognition, bestowed strictly for its impact on their social network.

Maybe we should charge a lot more for him, I pondered. At least then they'd have a reason to pay attention.

Michael and Henry went back to the drawing board and continued to rehearse. Not long after, Henry called me.

"I can't do this anymore," he said. "Michael keeps missing rehearsals. I think he only wants to date girls."

This was strange. Michael struck me as a determined artist.

"Are you sure? Could it be something else?"

"No, I don't think so. He's called me a few times with lame excuses about sleeping in. He's gotta show more interest if I'm going to keep helping him."

Remember that trust thing? Well, I trusted Henry implicitly. He had a good sense of what makes someone tick. As a loyal mainstay of our talent roster, he gave me no reason to doubt him. Plus, he wasn't getting paid for helping Michael; there was only the expectation of future work.

"OK, we have no contract, so cut him loose," I said. From then on it would be up to Bev to make his career happen on her own.

I never did find out why Michael missed rehearsals.

For the next couple of years I occasionally heard from Michael and Bev. She had managed to get him a lot of work with local bandleader legend Dal Richards, and he soon formed his own quintet. He landed a long-term lounge gig at a place called Babalu's. During that time he recorded his first album. But he was still only a *local* celebrity.

One of my good clients, a travel company, had heard the news about him and asked me to book him for a destination launch event at a local hotel. I did, this time for a significant amount of money. The event was for about six hundred travel agents with the intention of giving them an incentive to sell destination tours. The food was free. So was the booze. And the show was after dinner.

By now just about everyone in Vancouver knew who Michael Bublé was, so the audience got right into his show. Backed by his crack quintet, a nattily attired Michael was ripping through the old standards. As I watched from the side of the room, I could see that his lounge gig had improved his stage persona immeasurably. He was genuinely charismatic. However, he still had a few things to learn.

About forty-five minutes into his hour-long show, I noticed a fellow wandering through the seated audience in the direction of the stage. Michael noticed him about the same time. The guy was making mock dance moves and it looked like he was just grooving to the music. He got to the stage and said something to Michael to the effect that he wanted to get onstage. This was not right, I thought. Nothing happens unrehearsed on *my stage*. "Michael, don't do it," I yelled to myself, thinking Michael would wave him away. Too late. The guy was onstage in a flash.

Now, Michael was always a friendly performer. That was part of his charm. He didn't like to disappoint his audiences. He liked to connect. In this instance he connected too well.

Another yell to myself, "Don't give him the micro-phone!" Shit, he gave it to him. "Geez, you never do that, Michael. You've gotta stay in control."

A few mumbled words later, it was apparent that the guy was completely smashed. A friendly tussle ensued with Michael finally re-acquiring possession of the microphone.

"Thanks for helping me out up here, buddy," he said with a nervous smile as he began a new song. I think Michael actually believed the fellow would leave the stage. Not a chance.

I didn't know if the guy actually liked Michael or was just harassing him. Needless to say, he followed Michael around the stage trying to interact. Michael attempted to dance with him but the fellow wanted to take over. He would not leave.

Halfway through the song, I rushed over to my client and said, "We have to get him off."

"I'll find some big bruisers," she said. She found six. They got up onstage near the end of Michael's song. He stopped and let them do their thing.

The guy was small but belligerent. Nothing like a determined drunk. It took all six of them to forcibly hold him and pull him offstage, then unceremoniously dump him outside the hotel.

I could tell Michael was rattled, but he continued his set to the end, brushing off the incident with a casual comment, "I love my fans."

Looking back years later, I hoped that the incident might have been a small lesson for Michael in his meteoric rise to international stardom. Likewise, the early unpaid gig might have been a minuscule stepping stone for him. His emergence as one of the most charismatic stars in entertainment showed that he had indeed learned whatever lessons were offered to him, whether intentional or not. Although I played no part in Michael's eventual success, I was grateful Paul called me to the studio that day.

* * *

Rolf Harris was one of Ben's best friends.

Not long after recording his first hit, "Tie Me Kangaroo Down, Sport" in Australia in 1960, Rolf set sail for San Francisco on the P&O Lines ship, the *Oriana*, which made its first-ever landing in Vancouver en route. He never made it to San Francisco. If he had, in a convoluted way, even *my* world might have been different.

Ben met him for the first time as the ship landed in order to set up an appointment with the owner of the Cave Theatre Restaurant where Ben was working. They hit it off. At the time, both of them were neophytes in show business, but they offered value to each other. Ben knew promotion and Rolf could electrify an audience. Within a year, Rolf was touring western Canada playing to sold-out houses, with Ben as his Canadian agent and manager. They learned from each other as their business relationship blossomed into a long-term friendship, one that continues to this day.

Rolf returned to live in England permanently in 1962, and over the years occasionally crossed the Atlantic to tour with Ben in Canada.

By the time Ben and I were partners, there had not been many Canadian appearances, but one June a national philanthropic organization specifically asked for Rolf to perform at their national convention. I wanted to know more about him.

"What was it that first drew you to Rolf?" I asked.

"Rolf hated phoniness but he loved people," Ben said. "He was an extrovert and he knew how to relate to an audience. He looked them straight in the eyes and instantly connected. He would stay after shows and sign autographs until the last fan had left. He honestly appreciated them."

"What about his talent?" I asked.

"He had it by the bucketload. He was a champion swimmer in his early years. He was intelligent and multi-talented, especially musically. Really, though, he was an artist. His paintings are now worth hundreds of thousands of dollars each."

"Yeah, I've heard that. Wow, I'm looking forward to meeting him and seeing his show."

"You won't be disappointed."

When Rolf arrived, Ben and I accompanied him for lunch the day before the show to a small local restaurant. I was amazed at how many people of all ages knew him decades after his biggest hits, "Tie Me Kangaroo Down, Sport," "Jake the Peg," and "Six White Boomers," were released.

All eyes were on us as we entered the restaurant. Our waitress, a pretty twenty-something, would not even have been born when "Tie Me Kangaroo Down, Sport" was a hit.

"Aren't you Rolf Harris?" she asked.

"Yes, I am, darling. That's amazing. Thanks for asking. And don't you look smashing today."

She was awestruck. Rolf continued to kibitz with her as the room lit up with his presence. Ben looked at me as if to say, "See, I told you so."

Needless to say, we received premium service.

I was still to be more impressed. I had never seen Rolf perform live. His show exhibited his mind-boggling range of talent. He sang and played his unique invention the wobble board, a bendable piece of Masonite hardboard, plus a didgeridoo. And playing the didgeridoo is no easy feat. It requires immense breath control and a difficult-to-learn technique called circular breathing. Besides this, he cracked jokes and completed a giant painting of the Australian outback to music.

What irked me was the audience. They talked through the entire show, oblivious to him. Rolf soldiered on.

Ben and I were watching the show from the back of the room.

"What's the problem with these people?" I asked him.

"It's typical of this kind of crowd. They want the star to prove they can afford him, but they ignore him to prove they have power. It's the nature of the beast."

After a solid hour Rolf closed the show with "Tie Me Kangaroo." As he walked down the stage stairs, Ben and I greeted him. He was sweating. "That was a toughie," he said. No swearing, no derogatory comments. I couldn't believe how calm he was.

"God, that was one of the most difficult shows I've ever seen you do—and I've seen a lot," Ben said.

"Well, you know I've told you before," Rolf replied. "You just can't treat the audience like three-year-olds. Besides, I believe in their cause, no matter how they behave."

Now that was class.

It was this wonderful encounter with the artist known as Rolf that later influenced my ability to analyze the skills of performers. I knew from seeing him that the consummate entertainer had to possess three key ingredients: an unquestionable advanced skill at performing one's specialty, the inclusion of rehearsed but seemingly spontaneous humour in a show, and charismatic audience interaction. I had tremendous success with any such performers that I put on stage after that—and more importantly, with any shows that incorporated all these ingredients. And thanks to Rolf, I paid it forward to the students I later taught in colleges. What a great legacy!

Chapter Ten

Canada Day

I watched a tiny droplet of sweat trickle down Nancy's cheek, splat lusciously onto her chest at the edge of her blue dress, and roll into the recess between her breasts. I wanted to follow it.

The heat was getting to me. I blinked myself back to reality. "How's your water, Nance?" An attractive brunette, she was one of our three frontline vocalists.

"Almost time for another one." She smiled. "That's eight bottles today and counting."

Four or five hands reached for bottles at once. No wonder. It was 48° C and about 90% humidity. Monsoon season in Cambodia. July 1, 1993.

As everyone gulped water, I glanced at my watch for the umpteenth time, a nervous habit developed over the last few years before shows. 7:45 p.m. Fifteen minutes to show time.

I surveyed the audience and the setting, and thought about how we had come to be here.

It all started with a call a month earlier from an old military friend who was serving with UNTAC, the United Nations Transitional Authority in Cambodia. He needed to put together a Canada Day show fast for our troops serving there. Since my company was on the west coast and had performed on a successful military tour before, he came to me. I made calls to performers. Rehearsals were arranged. Airline bookings were made. Hotels were reserved. Thanks to military efficiency, we were ready to go in no time. A couple of long flights later via Hong Kong and Bangkok, and here we were. Our job? To motivate the troops so they could do *their* jobs helping to pull Cambodia out of the devastation caused years earlier by Pol Pot and the Khmer Rouge.

Those troops were now sitting in front of us, about two hundred of them. They were off-duty and dressed in shorts and t-shirts, their muscular bodies testament to the soldier's calling. They were primed for the show. Testosterone and beer-fuelled whooping echoed across the farmer's dirt field that formed our "theatre." Those still on duty wore battle fatigues and held automatic rifles at the ready on the rooftops of the farm's buildings. They didn't shout. Luckily, they didn't drink either.

It was an interesting setting. The word "quaint" would come to mind if the context of Cambodia's political situation was not so dreadful. But the troops had made the best of it. They had built a makeshift stage for us on the back of four flatbed trucks using sheets of teak plywood. For stage lighting, they had dug two large holes in front of the stage and placed tall poles with single, glaring site lights on top. They had found a giant Canadian flag and draped it across the back of the stage, which was formed by the cabs of the trucks. Most amazing, though, was their willingness to sleep in the heat. The promise of a local "dragon lady" to provide portable power for the sound system had not been kept. Sacrificing the air conditioning in their quarters was their last hope. Obviously, pretty girls and rock music rated much higher than keeping cool. We were impressed.

Tom, the musical director and band leader, was now preparing to go through the hour and a half show with the cast as we all sat in a circle in one of the farm's small barns just off to one side of the stage. It was our temporary green room. Everyone was already soaked from perspiration and the show hadn't even started. A carpet of empty water bottles covered the rough floor. As the producer I wouldn't be onstage but I had to know that the content would work for the audience, so I listened intently.

"OK, guys, this is it. This is why we're here." Tom started the pep talk and run-through.

"Yeah, God bless Canada Day," Billy the comedian and MC said.

"So just to review," Tom said, "we'll do the musical overture to open, then I'll intro Billy and he can bring the girls out for four songs. And vamp it up, girls. We wanna get these guys eating out of our hands as soon as possible. Remember, they're far from home and starved for love.

They've all been over here for at least six months with no wives or girlfriends."

"Don't worry, we'll make them want to eat more." Gina, the second vocalist, grinned and writhed in mock pleasure.

"Oh, yummyyy," moaned Dianne, the third vocalist. She was getting in the zone.

Nancy just smiled her perfect smile. I searched for another drop of sweat to follow.

"I'm on after them, right, for fifteen, twenty minutes?" Billy said.

"Right. You've gotta keep the momentum, man."

"No problemo, Thomas."

"After your stand-up, we come back for the Gloria Estefan and Miami Sound Machine set with the girls, plus the classic rock set. Then it's back to Billy and all of us for the Studs routine."

"So for Studs we bring up some lively guys from the audience?" Dianne asked.

"Right. Billy will announce the search and you three can go out and find two guys. After Studs, everyone's back for the finale. Remember, we do the two Expo songs to end—'Something's Happening Here' and 'Canada: This Is My Home.' Girls, you can pick up the small Canada flags and wave them. Interact with the guys in the audience."

It seemed like a good show, a mixture of comedy, hard-hitting rock, and emotion. The girls would be naturally popular with the army boys, all in their twenties.

Tom said, "Any questions?"

"Hey, Doug, just keep the water coming, OK?" Gina said.

"You got it," I said.

"Let's do it, then!" Tom said, sounding more like a football coach than a band leader.

Everyone walked over to the stage. The band went up and turned their instruments on while the girls and Billy stood by the stairs. I waited with them.

It was time. But a hint of worry nagged me.

Worrying was part of my job. It's what took care of loose ends.

Although this was only our second—and last—day in Cambodia, what we had encountered in the short time here had me wondering if even these highly seasoned performers would be able to pull themselves out of a serious funk and deliver a great show. Why?

First, the show was outdoors and this evening's sky was menacing. If it rained we knew from a downpour in the afternoon that it would not be a light drizzle. Monsoons didn't drizzle; they deluged. There was always a flood somewhere. Stage lighting and sound systems did not take kindly to such soakings. Neither did costumes like blue sequined dresses. Neither did three attractive singers with makeup and styled hair. I prayed that Cambodia's rain gods would be kind. There was no alternative.

Second, our show "venue" was depressing. A small farm, it lay about ten kilometres from the capital of Phnom Penh. It was home to the Canadian peacekeepers. The soldiers had given us a tour of it the day before. We hit all the highlights. Razor wire perimeter fence. Sandbagged bunkers. Round-the-clock armed guards. As the tour ended, our escort officer, Captain Dan, emerged from a bunker with a large glass jar.

"We've collected these from the men's quarters and the bunkers." The jar was full of what looked like large cobras and several other unattractive reptiles, all deceased and drifting in formaldehyde. "Be careful where you walk and keep your eyes open. They're all poisonous."

We glanced around our feet.

Billy said, "I guess cow patties are the least of our worries on this farm."

Nervous laughter.

"Oh, and I almost forgot," Captain Dan said. "If you hear gunshots in the distance, it's most likely some remnants of Khmer Rouge trying to disrupt things. Don't worry, though, we're well protected."

"Yeah, no problem," Tom said. Nancy's eyes got bigger and her jaw dropped. The other two girls gasped. The guys just raised their eyebrows and tried to look cool.

But there was no more nervous laughter.

A faint memory of Nancy's father shouting at me to protect her and the other performers on this trip suddenly grew stronger. I was responsible for anything and everything that happened to them.

"Great to be here. Thanks for the tour, Captain Dan," I said, as calmly as possible.

Fortunately, what the troops had done with this small piece of real estate between yesterday and today went a long way to easing my concerns about it.

What we had seen this morning, though, formed the most serious reason I was worried.

Shortly after breakfast in our tiny—the elevator could accommodate one person and a suitcase—but adequate hotel in downtown Phnom Penh, Captain Dan had shown up promptly at 0900 hours with a small school bus to take us around the city. It was the army's way of making us feel welcome.

Outside the hotel, the face of poverty and hopelessness slammed into us. Bombed-out shells of once-magnificent homes and stately government offices competed for attention with the din of shouting, incessant car horns, and roaring motorcycles. There were no traffic lights and shockingly few policemen. Traffic control was more a game of chicken than rule-governed.

From the sidewalks, mournful eyes followed our rattling bus. Limbless bodies hobbled pitifully or sat forlornly.

We gawked out the windows. We definitely weren't in Vancouver anymore.

Captain Dan sensed our shock. "This country is in massive upheaval now. Many of those people out there have lost arms and legs to land mines. They have no way to earn a living."

"It's so sad," Dianne said. "And all those wrecked buildings, too."

"Most of the bombed-out buildings you see were constructed by the French during the period Cambodia was a French protectorate from 1863 to 1953."

"What happened to everything?" Dianne said.

"Pol Pot and the Khmer Rouge. That's what happened."

"I've heard of him. He was a bad dude, right?" Billy said.

"Yup. Seriously evil. In 1975 he brought in a warped version of communism. Khmer Rouge was the name of his party. They were trying to create an agrarian society and literally exterminated around two million people, pretty well anyone with an education or who even remotely *looked* educated, like doctors, teachers, engineers, lawyers. It's been said that anyone wearing eyeglasses was killed."

Several of us wearing them looked askance. "Guess *we'd* all be gone," I said.

"You would be for sure," Captain Dan said.

"So why are Canadians here, then?" Tom said.

"Good question. Last year the United Nations created UNTAC. Its purpose is to rebuild the country and we're part of it. Last month we monitored the first free elections in many years, and we're also teaching the Cambodians how to disarm land mines."

"Were the elections successful?" Tom said.

"We think so. Only time will tell if the government will be stable."

In a few minutes we arrived at our first stop, a simple, three-storey, institutional white building. The soft morning sun warmed the gardens around it. It looked innocent. It wasn't.

Captain Dan announced, "This is Tuol Sleng. It used to be a high school, but the Khmer Rouge turned it into a prison. It's an important part of recent Cambodian history. Here's our guide, Samnang. He'll take us around. Feel free to ask him questions."

We started our tour. The first few rooms were neat and tidy with colourful tiled floors, but something was different. "The rooms seem too small to be classrooms," Dianne said. "They look more like hotel rooms."

Samnang responded with a heavy accent, "Khmer Rouge brick up real classrooms, turn into 'bedrooms,' torture chambers. They want extract confession from prisoners that they against revolution; find excuse to kill them. You look close."

We did. With each room new information was revealed.

One near the beginning of the tour offered a set of poorly translated "regulations" that must have struck terror into the hearts of those arriving, and a glimpse into what awaited them in their "bedrooms." The final regulation spelled out the consequences of not obeying instructions.

"If you disobey any point of my regulations you shall get either ten lashes or five shocks of electric discharge."

"Oh my god!" Gina said.

"Those poor people. Whatever became of them?" Nancy was an empathizer.

"Most, they die," Samnang said. "Lots go to Killing Fields."

"How many people came here, then?" Nancy said.

"We think, hmm, maybe twenty thousand," Samnang said. "I one of lucky twelve who survive." He pointed to his left eye, partly shut. "Blind this eye," he said, while starting to unbutton his shirt, exposing his gaunt brown torso. His back was covered with dozens of long-healed, purple welts, his chest with ugly red scars. "Khmer Rouge do this," he said, turning around. "Many times, over and over, lashes on back, electric shocks on front. Right here, this building."

We looked at each other in silent disbelief and continued through the gruesome displays.

Toward the end, Samnang drew our attention to a cot in the middle of one room.

"This room left exactly as day prison close. See dark marks on floor under bed? That blood from prisoner who bleed to death from knife wound."

I had visited a Nazi concentration camp in Alsace-Lorraine years before. This was just as bad, maybe worse.

The tour finished in a room with a glass case filled with instruments of torture and a wall map of Cambodia filled with skulls.

This was not the best way to get everyone in a positive frame of mind, I thought. I was starting to wonder how I would get them back into "show mode" for the evening.

Billy tried to lift our spirits as we reboarded the bus. "Well, this has really changed my view of high school forever. I knew it was hard, but this is crazy."

We all managed slight smiles. They quickly evaporated as Captain Dan said almost cheerily, "Next stop, the Killing Fields."

South of the city, lush green rice paddies were interspersed with small villages of stilted houses. Nowhere was there a hint of the horror that had enveloped Cambodia in the late 70s. As we rumbled toward our destination, the last few kilometres on a pot-holed dirt road, it was Nancy who noticed an opportunity.

"Look at all those kids. Stop the bus. I want to talk to them," she said, a sense of urgency in her voice. We lurched to a stop in front of several ramshackle houses.

She got out and was engulfed in a sea of giggling, tawny-skinned children. A few were missing limbs. It didn't matter. They were kids and kids do what kids want to do. Nancy was handing out souvenir Canada pins to each one. She beamed from ear to ear and the kids felt her happiness. It was the first time I'd seen such joyful innocence since we arrived in Cambodia. Perhaps a tiny ray of hope still shone within this country. I hoped that some of it was absorbed by our group.

The pure irony, however, was not lost. We were less than a kilometre from the Killing Fields.

"Choeung Ek, the location's real name," Captain Dan pointed out as we approached, "used to be an orchard. It was here that the final, most notorious brutalities of the Khmer Rouge regime took place."

It was still sunny as we stepped off the bus near an attractive, glass-walled Buddhist *stupa*. Around it were peaceful-looking fields interspersed with old trees. As we had come to realize, though, outward appearances usually hid sinister truths.

Our guide, Nimol, quickly proved it. "Welcome," he said. "I know much about this place. Stupa seventeen storeys high. It contain skulls of many who die here, almost nine thousand."

Nimol was younger than our Tuol Sleng guide, perhaps late teens or early twenties. I wondered how he could have known about what happened. It was over eighteen years ago.

He continued. "My family—parents, five brothers and sisters—all die here. I'm only one to live, because I was very small child when Khmer Rouge come, and guards make friends with me."

"What happened to all of them?" Dianne said.

"My father was doctor, so they put him and my mother in Tuol Sleng, then bring whole family to Choeung Ek after two months. Come over here and you see what happen."

We followed him around some large open pits, all with signs indicating they were mass graves. I noticed something odd about the dirt and picked up a handful. Only it wasn't just dirt. In it were countless chunks of human bone, teeth, and clothing. The entire field was the same.

Soon Nimol came to an imposing tree. Part way up the trunk were numerous horizontal gashes in the bark. As he stood with his back to the tree, it was obvious that the gashes were at neck height.

"Victims stand here," he said. Then he took one step out, "and ..." He turned and swung his arms toward the tree.

He paused, remembering. "Axes save ammunition."

We stood quietly for a long time, trying to imagine the horror of watching our families executed before our eyes.

The return trip to our hotel was mercifully short. I sensed that everyone wanted to just rest and absorb what they'd seen. They needed down time. A question on my own mind—and no doubt on everyone else's—was *why* we had seen it, especially with our imminent show. After all, we were performers, not social engineers. I just had to trust that the army had a reason, although unexplained and not obvious yet.

As the bus pulled to a stop in front of our hotel, Captain Dan gave us a curious warning. "By the way, if you're out on the street, don't stray too far and don't accept any gifts from the locals. You never know what they might be."

I immediately thought this might mean something explosive, then leading the way, I stepped off the bus.

Suddenly she was there. A pretty, young Cambodian girl, no more than eighteen. She held a bundle of cloths in her arms and thrust them at me, pleading, *"Monsieur, s'il vous plaît prendre mon bébé. Donnez-lui une vie meilleure."* My god, it was a baby!

Remembering Captain Dan's words, I continued past her, trying not to look upset. Everyone else put their heads down and avoided eye contact with her. The girl departed along the sidewalk in tears, grief-stricken.

Inside the hotel, *our* girls all talked at once.

"How could anyone do that, just hand over your baby to a complete stranger?"

"I could *never* do that."

I tried to calm things down. "Look, everyone, you know there's nothing we can do about what we just saw. It's been pretty much a downer this morning. But we have a job to do tonight and we need to get focused. You're on your own for the afternoon. Try to get some rest. We'll meet in the lobby for our departure at six o'clock." I knew they would be having trouble.

I didn't rest at all.

The show began slowly. A few whistles greeted the girls but nothing startling. I had a sinking feeling that they were not yet out of their funk. The soldiers weren't exactly eating out of their hands.

Then it was Billy's turn. A short, stand-up routine should get the audience going, I thought. After all, I'd sat next to him on the airplane to Bangkok, and he'd kept me in stitches for fifteen hours.

A couple of jokes. Nothing.

A couple more and the heckling started.

"Lame jokes, man," came a voice from the rear.

Billy paused for a split second. "Hey, buddy, you oughta save your breath. You'll need it later to blow up your inflatable date."

"Come on, man, you can do better. Give us some funny stuff," another soldier yelled.

"That's okay, pal. I remember when I had *my* first beer." Billy then managed one more story out of his routine before the shouts resurfaced.

"What kind of story was that? My grandmother can do better."

But no moss grew on Billy's turf. "Look, I've only got twenty minutes to make a fool out of myself and you have the rest of your life, so shut up." Then, as if to a hidden sidekick, "This is why some animals eat their young."

Finally it hit me. Billy was in his element. He was a club comic. His arsenal was limitless. After a few more exchanges, and realizing Billy was not about to give an inch, the soldiers stood up and cheered. He'd won them over.

Things got easier and my anxiety lowered a notch.

By the end of the Miami Sound Machine set, most of the audience was standing and shouting. The girls loved the attention and settled in, revving up the soldiers with flirtatious exchanges.

The Studs routine was a takeoff on the popular 90s TV dating game. The girls pulled a couple of handsome guys up to the stage. Billy asked them questions about their fictitious dates with the three girls. This brought most of the audience to the edge of the stage to egg on their buddies.

"Stud #1, what did you like physically about your date with Gina?" Billy began.

"She had beautiful, um, eyes?" Stud #1 felt his pecs. His buddies roared.

"Stud #2, what did you whisper in Nancy's ear when you took her home?"

"Want to come up and see my etchings?" Stud #2 stood up and rotated his pelvis. Another roar from *his* supporters.

"Stud #1, where did you take Dianne for your date?"

"Well, we took one of the pickup trucks and made out by the Mekong River. I took my rifle along to protect her. She loved my gun."

The entire audience went crazy. Billy hardly had to crack a joke. The guys were naturals. After more questions, the girls gave paper hearts to both and announced the contest a draw.

It was obvious a bond had formed between the performers and the soldiers. My anxiety evaporated.

Then came the finale.

The second song, "I'm Gonna Be 500 Miles" by the Proclaimers, caught the rest of the diehards, who now rushed up to the stage to join their friends. I realized something special was happening but I couldn't put my finger on it.

As I stood by the stage, I noticed six guys who had spent the whole show so far sitting on top of the building that had been our green room. They had draped a large Canadian flag over the roof and now picked it up, jumped off the roof, and began to run around the field with it just as our last two patriotic songs began. The troops by the stage were now screaming and shouting uncontrollably, waving their arms in the air.

"We love you girls."

"We love Canada."

The girls completely fell apart. They could barely finish the songs.

When they came off stage at the end, their makeup had disappeared in a flood of tears. Their costumes were drenched in sweat.

Trying to swallow away the largest lump I had ever had in my throat, I managed only a feeble "Fabulous show, everyone." We hardly had time to hug each other before the onslaught of soldiers.

They mobbed the girls and the band. They were crying—and hugging each other—saying, "I love you, man." Big bruisers of men, reduced to sobs.

The picture was wrong. What had just happened? Sure, the troops were living half a world away from normal, but there was more to it.

A mental switch clicked on. This show was not just for the troops. It was for Cambodia: for Samnang, for Nimol, for the laughing kids, for the young mother, for the countless victims of the Khmer Rouge. It was about the human spirit and the will to help others in agony. That is what Canada was doing and our band of entertainers was helping in our own small way. It was a lesson that could only have hit home by realizing what the Canadians were up against and what had happened in Cambodia's past. The tours we had taken suddenly made ultimate sense. I was never so proud of my country as at that moment, nor so happy to be born Canadian. I knew my performers felt the same.

A higher power was surely at work here.

I have never before or since felt such deep emotion.

In later years my company was honoured to produce tours for Canadian troops in other war-torn countries, including Bosnia and Afghanistan. To a person, every performer said that their experience was life-changing.

We had connected.

About the Author

After serving twenty-two years in the Canadian Armed Forces as an aeronautical engineer, Doug Matthews began his second career in the entertainment industry when he joined Pacific Show Productions, located in Vancouver, Canada, in 1985. This company produced special events and entertainment in Canada and overseas for many diverse clients. These included: original musical theatre productions in Barkerville, B.C.; the millennium First Night celebrations in Vancouver, B.C.; the annual Leo Awards for B.C. film and television; and entertainment show tours for the Canadian Armed Forces to the Arctic, Afghanistan, Bosnia, Cambodia, Egypt, and Israel. Pacific Show Productions was regularly nominated for special event awards both in Canada and the United States and won several under his leadership. The company was sold in 2004.

Doug has been writing since he was in the air force. His first book was a self-published work on special events,

How to Create Fantasies and Win Accolades: A Practical Guide to Planning Special Events, which received critical acclaim in the United States and Canada. Another two books on event production entitled *Special Event Production, Part One: The Process* and *Special Event Production, Part Two: The Resources* were published by Elsevier in 2008 and are currently marketed around the English-speaking world.

Made in the USA
Charleston, SC
17 May 2014